MILPITAS

The Century of 'Little Cornfields'
1852-1952

BY
PATRICIA LOOMIS

MILPITAS HISTORICAL SOCIETY
Milpitas, California

Milpitas Historical Society
Milpitas, California

Published by Milpitas Historical Society
40 N. Milpitas Blvd., Milpitas, California 95035

Second Edition
    The First Edition, ISBN 0-93508907-1, was published by the
    California History Center, Cupertino, California in 1986.

ISBN 0-9678333-1-0 (paper) – $8.00
Library of Congress Card Number: 00-104389

ISBN 0-9678333-1-0

9 780967 833316

5 0 8 0 0

Foreword

In its first thousands of years, Milpitas could not be distinguished from the rest of the San Francisco Bay area.

Costonoan Indians had camped beside the streams, hunted rabbits and deer, pounded acorns into meal in holes in rocks. By the time our story starts in the 1850s, the Indians had nearly disappeared, the Mexican period was over and California had become a state.

Some lines had been drawn on the land separating one huge rancho from another. Distinguished by landmarks such as a large tree, the Californios' boundaries did not make much impression on the land. Neither did the cattle they raised for they roamed over the hundreds of acres of grasslands without fences, and ranching was not intensive.

De Anza had explored the paths, padres strode beneath olive trees shading the path between Mission San Jose and Mission Santa Clara. The place on the Penitencia Creek to be called Milpitas was just a spot on the path even in the early 1800s.

There were a few adobes built then, homes of Californios, one of which —the Alviso adobe— survives intact and another —the Tularcitos adobe—which was reconstructed.

This easy-going (for the period) kind of life was swept away when the Yankees arrived. It is this period described by Pat Loomis in the following pages.

Pat Loomis's curiosity had been piqued when, as a reporter for the *San Jose News*, she had interviewed descendants of the early settlers. Roads were just beginning to be built during that time. Named after the more prominent settlers—Weller, Abel, Evans and others Ms. Loomis wrote about in a series called "Signposts".

Her San Jose "Signposts" were published in a book by

the same name by the San Jose Historical Museum Association. When she was approached by the Milpitas Historical Society to do a similar book for Milpitas, she had retired from the *San Jose News*. With more time at her disposal, she began to polish her already published material about Milpitas and soon found rather than a simple rewriting and fact-checking, she had a full scale research job.

Her reporter's instincts for facts led her on to find little-known diaries and newspaper writing during the time and set it in a framework of the major state and national events of the time.

Ms. Loomis had written a readable book about the one hundred years leading to the city's incorporation that will be valuable to the citizens of the community from elementary students to elder statesmen.

Elaine Levine

Author's Note

Some 48 years have passed since we ended the story of Milpitas' first 100 years.

Now (2000) it is time to reprint "Milpitas – The Century of 'Little Cornfields'" and a brief update is necessary.

In the first century, 1852-1952, agriculture was the reason for the little settlement strung along Main Street, the local name for the two-lane highway linking San Jose and Oakland.

Decades rolled by with little change until 1953 when Ford Motor Company picked a hunk of Western Pacific Railroad land to build its multi-million dollar plant.

Suddenly it was a new era. Milpitas became an incorporated city in January, 1954 and was on its way to becoming one of the fastest growing cities in the nation.

Milpitas did not grow haphazardly along old wagon roads and cow paths as many California communities had done. It expanded along lines of master plans well-conceived by community leaders and involved citizens.

Wide streets were laid out, high quality residential developments (including Sunnyhills, one of the nation's first integrated subdivisions) were interspersed with industrial and recreational parks and commercial buildings.

Ford remained the major industrial plant in the city until its close in 1983, but by then high tech industries had moved in, drawn by cheap land and the availability of utilities, freeways, two railroads and housing for employees in a family-oriented new city.

From less than a thousand residents in a tiny farming community, Milpitas' population reached 50,000 by the city's 40th birthday.

The face of Milpitas had changed dramatically. Multi-storied hotels and industrial plants were creating a skyline by the early 1990's. The Ford Plant was replaced by the largest outlet mall in Northern California and a very large regional shopping center was build on fertile farmland in the northwest corner of the city.

The "little cornfields," along with the grain fields, asparagus and strawberry patches, had disappeared. The Fat Boy Barbecue, Cracolice's drug store and Cusiz's Ford agency were gone from Main Street.

Calaveras Road had been elevated to "boulevard" status, and modern homes spread over the hayfields of Samuel Ayer and John Dempsey.

The eastern foothills still follow the seasons, turning from green to golden brown with only a few windows reflecting the afternoon sun, but even the most imaginative of early settlers would never have visualized the view from Evans Road down into the valley in the 1990's.

The old history has been kept alive on streets named Barber, Dempsey, Jacklin, Sinott and Windsor, and a 1990 inventory listed more than 40 historical sites to remind newcomers of Milpitas' history.

Growth and change is expected to continue well into the 21st century and future historians will have much to write about.

– Patricia Loomis

Index to Photos & Illustrations

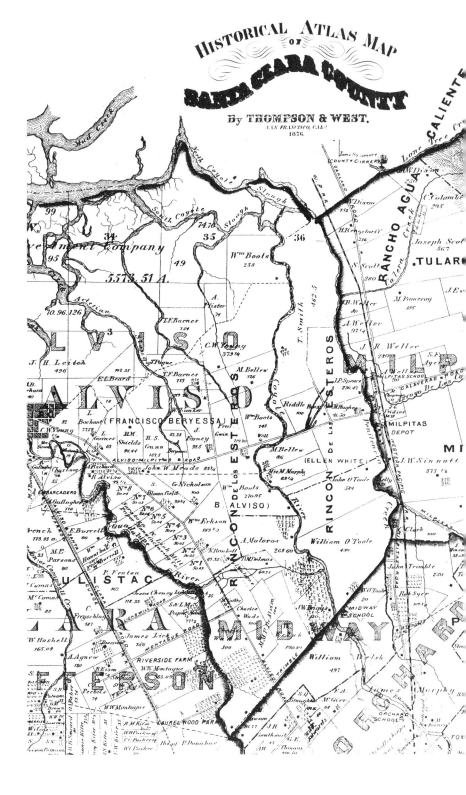

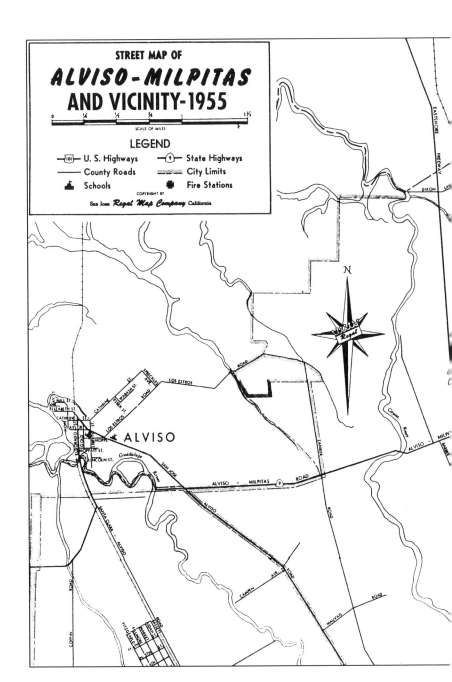

STREET MAP OF
ALVISO-MILPITAS
AND VICINITY-1955

SCALE OF MILES

LEGEND

—101— U. S. Highways   —9— State Highways
——— County Roads   City Limits
Schools   Fire Stations

COPYRIGHT BY
San Jose *Regal Map Company* California

N

ALVISO

ALVISO - MILPITAS ROAD

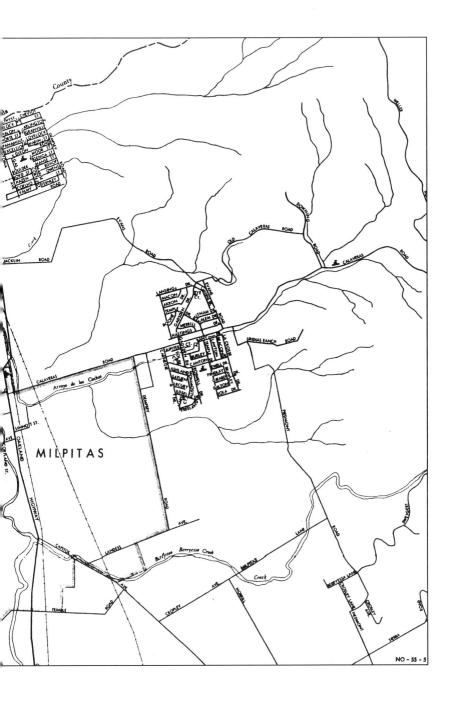

MILPITAS

ACKNOWLEDGEMENTS

First Edition:

Elaine Levine, Anne Campbell Smith, Bart Sepulveda, Bob McGuire, Ed Cavallini, Milpitas Library, City of Milpitas, Edward Chong, California History Center, San Jose Historical Museum, San Jose Mercury, San Francisco Water Co., and the family of Gene Vennum.

Second Edition:

Dean Baird, Elaine Traughber, Jeanne and Ed Cavallini.

Chapter I

An Irishman named Michael Hughes cleared a patch of tall mustard and built a house beside the dirt road that stretched between Mission San Jose and the pueblo of the same name.

This was in 1852 and was, history tells us, the first building constructed on the site of the town of Milpitas. However, it is more than likely Hughes' few distant neighbors failed to realize the historic significance of his endeavor.

Even three years later, in 1855, when the first store was built nearby, there was little to indicate this was the beginning of a permanent town. It was only the steady influx of settlers coming in later to farm the rich land that gave the little settlement its place in history.

Long before Hughes and his neighbors arrived, bare feet of Indians, boots of Spanish explorers and the moccasins of fur trappers had made the first faint trails across the plain and into the hills.

Then came the families with the Spanish names of Higuera and Alviso who claimed the land and built their adobe haciendas back against the foothills.

They built no fences and their cattle and horses roamed with the elk and antelope, grazing under the huge oak trees and drinking from streams named Arroyo de los Coches, Penitencia and Coyote.

1

Horseback travel and the wooden wheels of the creaking carretas had widened the road between the mission and the pueblo, which had been joined near a bend in the Penitencia east of the Coyote by a set of ruts coming in from the Alviso landing on the bay.

Although some of the original settlers, the Indians, remained to work for the rancheros, most of them were crowded out as their fishing and hunting grounds were invaded with the parcelling out of great chunks of the land stretching from the south edge of the bay up into the hills beyond Mission San Jose and then south to take in the plains along the Coyote.

Of the three great ranchos, the one named Milpitas was chosen as the future site of the town that would have the same name. Michael Hughes had built his house in the northwest sector of the 4,457.66 acres granted to Jose Maria Alviso in 1835 by the Mexican governor Jose Castro. The name is a Nahuatl (Aztec) word meaning "little cornfields" or gardens, and it was to be prophetic.

To the north across Arroyo de los Coches was Rancho Tularcitos ("little tule thickets"), extending from Penitencia Creek up into the eastern hills. Its 4,394.35 acres were granted to Jose Higuera in 1821 by Pablo Vincente de Sola, last Spanish governor of Alta California, and confirmed in 1839 by Governor Juan Bautista Alvarado under the laws of Mexico.

Still farther north along the line that later would mark the boundary between Santa Clara and Alameda Counties was the 9,563.87-acre spread granted to Fulgencio Higuera by Governor Alvarado in 1839. It was known as Agua Caliente ("hot water") because of warm springs in the foothills south of Mission San Jose.

In 1850 the Court of Sessions meeting in San Jose, seat of newly-created Santa Clara County, decreed the county's first public thoroughfare would be the Mission Road.

Alviso adobe on Piedmont Road about 1918. Florence Lee (Ogier) Hawley photo.

3

Remains of Higuera adobe 1948.

4

Following the existing trail, the road, according to the court's description, began at San Jose and went northeast past James Murphy's ranch and Fulgencia Higuera's Agua Caliente through Mission San Jose to the county line, which at that time was Alameda Creek.

The new settlers coming to the area found a park-like plain with its giant oaks and the springtime yellow of mustard so tall the wild game and cattle were lost in it.

It was as Death Valley pioneer William Lewis Manly described, the mustard stalks so strong ground squirrels climbed them "to get a better view."

Early morning and at dusk great flocks of ducks and geese threw shadows on the plain. No city lights dimmed the stars at night, the quiet broken only by the cry of an owl or the bark of a coyote.

The coming of the wagon emigrants was to change the look of the land, the game moving back into the hills with the springtime plowing and the sound of hammers as houses and barns went up.

Other changes marked this early beginning.

The days of the great ranchos were ending. Portions of these vast estates were being sold and squatters were taking up other chunks of them in the belief the land belonged to the government.

Land titles were to plague the newcomer as well as the owners of the great rancheros for years to come.

Some of the earliest settlers came from the gold fields in the Sierra foothills, willing to trade a plow for a pick and shovel after months of standing in frigid mountain streams while the top half of them burned in the fierce sun.

Many of these miners came from farms beyond the Missouri, and some had been teachers, lawyers, storekeepers and blacksmiths. Some came by horseback or wagon train across plains and mountains and others chose the sea route, suffering the hardships and fevers of Panama.

A few brought their families, and others came alone or with friends they had met en route or in the mining camps.

Some came from other lands, looking for a new and better life away from the wars of Europe and the famine of Ireland.

Most were young.

Few were as rich as the Martin Murphy clan whose great ranches hopscotched the length of Santa Clara County and spread elsewhere in Central California. The family had come west in 1844 with the first emigrant party to bring wagons over the Sierra. Martin Murphy, Jr. bought a big piece of Rancho Milpitas spreading out from the hills north of Berryessa Creek, and James Murphy acquired land east of the Mission Road in an area known as Berryessa.

Other settlers rode into the hills to lay claim to land in the valley called Calaveras ("skulls"). Records indicate as early as 1850 men named William Chipman, Charles Crosner, M.R. and Wilson Brown, William Daniels and two recorded only as Rix and Crote, were in the valley.

Little or nothing is known of them and they did not stay long, selling to others looking for land to farm.

William Daniels, native of England who had come overland with the westward migration of 1846, left the little valley to become a prominent horticulturist and justice of the peace in San Jose Township. He was president of the San Jose and Alviso Turnpike Road from 1861 to 1863 when it was purchased by the county and declared a public road.

Of Wilson Brown, we know he stayed around long enough to become the second justice of the peace of Milpitas Township in 1863.

Down on the flatlands near Hughes' house built of redwood hauled down from the forested western mountains, also settled the brothers Abraham and Joseph

Weller from New Jersey, who like Hughes had come from "the states" by the sea route. The Wellers had spent a couple of years mining at Coloma before deciding to settle in the Santa Clara Valley in 1852.

This was also the year Charles Clark came from Ohio with his family, and Joseph Scott and two other men bought 3,000 acres of Rancho Agua Caliente for $3 an acre. The land was then in Santa Clara County, but the following year it shifted over the line with the creation of Alameda County out of parts of Contra Costa and Santa Clara Counties.

The Josiah Evans family also came from Ohio, but it took them nearly four years to reach the Santa Clara Valley. They started for the California gold fields in 1849, but laid over until the spring of 1850 in St. Joseph, Missouri because of a cholera epidemic raging on the plains. Their wagons made it over the Sierras in October, and the family went to the mines on the Feather River.

Evans established a store and hotel at a place which became known as Evansville in Butte County, but after a year he became a drover and trader back on the trail into California, buying the trail-weary stock of overland immigrants and driving them to the "sink" of the Humboldt River where he fattened them before pushing them over the mountains into California to sell.

The Evans family bought 800 acres of Rancho Tularcitos in 1853. They would buy the land a second time before getting a clear title.

Up in Calaveras Valley, Dudley Wells and Nicholas Roland Harris had wandered over from the gold country and settled down to farming by late 1853. They had come overland the previous year with another early Milpitas resident, Alfred French, who was to establish Milpitas' first hotel. Harris was to serve several years as sheriff of Santa Clara County.

Hughes' residence was the first frame house in Milpitas. The histories do not tell us what kind of shelter Charles Clark built for his family that same year, but at least one of the old history books claims bachelor Joseph Weller built the second frame house in the area.

There was still no settlement at the crossroads on the Mission Road, the few settlers traveling to Alviso or San Jose for supplies. But it was getting almost crowded up in the Calaveras Valley.

In February, 1855, a petition was presented to the county supervisors asking for a county road out of the hills and across the valley to Alviso, noting "more than 60 families" living in the little valley.

Helping to swell this population, and affixing their names to the petition were four ex-gold miners from New York: John T. Sherman, Alexander Campbell, John S. and Jesse Stuart.

With the new road and all the traffic from the hills, the beginnings of a town began showing up on the flatlands.

Frederick Creighton, native of England who came to California with the '49ers, and whose name sometimes appears as Crighton, built a store at the crossroads of Mission Road and the new road which connected Calaveras Valley with the Alviso landing. This is believed to be the first business building on the townsite, and was followed soon after by a blacksmith shop operated by Abraham Weller. Also, in 1855, Joseph Weller (who taught school in New York), Robert Hutchinson of Alviso and Thomas Whitten organized a subscription school. At this time the Milpitas area was part of Alviso township and school district.

A school was completed in 1856, a one-room building 24 by 30 feet, costing some $600.

It was in this year that Louis and Pierre Pellier introduced the little French plum that was to become the basis of Santa Clara County's world-famed prune industry for nearly a century.

Also in 1856 the Republican Party was organized in Santa Clara County and Milpitans among its founders included Augustus Rathbone, Joseph R. and Abraham Weller, Josiah Evans, Hiram Pomeroy and William Boots.

The Overland Mail Co. was organized by John Butterfield in 1857 and mail service from St. Louis to San Francisco began the following year.

On May 31, 1858, a post office was established in Creighton's store.

The name "Milpitas" was affixed to the post office, suggested, some early writers claim, by Joseph Weller as opposed to "Penitencia," a name some of the residents had been using to refer to the crossroads community.

Creighton was Milpitas' first postmaster and Joe Weller was assistant.

A hotel had been built in 1857, operated briefly by one James Kinney and then taken over by Alfred French, the man from Ohio who had come overland with Calaveras farmers Harris and Wells.

Meanwhile, wagons continued to bring new settlers to the area.

The John Sinnott family (relatives of the Murphys) came over from Mountain View where they had been farming since coming to California from Canada in 1851.

Henry Rengstorff, native of Germany and California pioneer of 1851, settled on land up near the new county line. Canadian Robert Welch in 1856 bought 188 acres in the southwest corner of Rancho Milpitas.

By the late 1850's, brothers named Baker had established a landing just over the county line at a place called Harrisburg, and Milpitas had become a stage stop on the line between San Jose and Oakland.

Hiram Pomeroy, native of Indiana who had been mining up at Jamison Creek in Plumas County, took up a pre-empted claim of 160 acres in Calaveras Valley, followed by a Scot named John Carrick who brought his family,

The Jacob Miller family, which first settled in Calaveras Valley, moved back over the hill to become possibly the first settlers in the smaller Laguna Valley, the area which a century later would become part of Ed Levin County Park.

The Millers (from Indiana) were neighbors of Frederick Pfeifle, a German immigrant who settled in the area in 1858, became a teamster and married Sarah Miller, daughter of Jacob.

Pfeifle had come from Michigan by the sea route and aboard ship met Proctor Wells, who was coming out to join his brother, Dudley.

In an interview with Pfeifle on his 91st birthday, published in the San Jose Mercury in 1928, he said he decided to tag along with Wells when they arrived in San Francisco. The two young men boarded a steamer to Alviso and then walked to Milpitas where they were met by Proctor's brother.

Pfeifle described Milpitas in 1858 as "a thriving village of two adobe saloons and a blacksmith shop." (One of the saloons undoubtedly was Creighton's store which sold everthing from canned goods to clothing, lamp chimneys and harness, and which also kept a bar for thirsty shoppers and travelers.)

Proctor Wells was a carpenter, but decided to try farming and bought a piece of land near his brother. However, after two nearly fatal brushes with wild animals, he was persuaded to return to carpentry and civilization.

His biography in J.M. Guinn's "History of the State of California and Biographic Record of Coast Counties,

10

California," published in 1904, gives a dramatic account of attacks by wild cattle and a lion.

The latter episode is reprinted here partly because of Guinn's wonderfully outrageous style of writing.

"One night as he (Proctor) was going home, he spied a large California lion lying on a limb of a tree which he was just about to pass under. He was but seven yards distance from the beast, and thoughts of home, of his mother, and of the ginger cookies that she used to make when he was a boy passed through his mind.

"His blood stopped circulating, his pulse ceased to beat, and his heart stood still, " Quinn continues.

"When he came to his senses, Mr. Wells began to walk backward, continuing for fifteen yards, when he jumped the creek, and made his way to Bulwer's (probably J.M. Boulware, who had a farm in Calaveras Valley at this time).

"Mr. Bulwer seized his rifle, mounted his blooded horse, and went in pursuit of the lion, which he shot and brought home." The big cat measured nine feet, seven inches, according to Guinn.

Proctor Wells didn't last a year farming, but moved to San Jose where he became a building contractor, constructing many residences and business buildings, as well as the ornate 1888 City Hall that graced South Market Street for more than 60 years.

By this time Augustus Rathbone, native of Rhode Island, had opened a second store (with saloon) in Milpitas, and Joseph Weller was operating a blacksmith shop (possibly with his brother), as well as serving as school trustee, farming, and organizing his neighbors in the repair of roads.

Alfred Doten, a New Englander who came to California in the gold rush of '49, lived in the Milpitas area from 1858 until the spring of 1863. He kept a day-by-day diary which was published by the University of Nevada Press in 1973, and which provides glimpses of life in Milpitas and the whole of Santa Clara County in this early period.

Doten did his trading at Creighton's and Rathbone's, and had farm equipment repaired at Weller's blacksmith shop.

One evening in November, 1858, Doten and his friend Abram Harris (Alameda County lawyer who had bought part of Agua Caliente rancho and given his name to the settlement on the Mission Road, later known as Warm Springs) stopped by Rathbone's with a box of eggs Harris was selling to the storekeepers.

"Some half dozen of them were cracked," Doten wrote in his diary, "so we got Rathbone to make an egg-nogg (sic) for us. . . made a nice one with Jamaica rum in it."

Four days prior to this visit Doten was in Milpitas to assess the damage from the earthquake of November 25, and notes that Rathbone suffered the most. His list of the items thrown from the shelves and broken--preserved fruits, brandied peaches, wines, crockery and glass--give an idea of what was sold in the general stores of the late 1850s.

He mentions working with O.H.P. Vennum and others of the Berryessa district on a road crew repairing Mission Road in April, 1859, digging a deep ditch along the edge to drain the water off into the Penitencia Creek. Joseph Weller was in charge of the crew and there were some 20 working with four teams and scrapers.

"Weller stood treat to 2 bottles of whiskey" when the work was finished, Doten wrote.

The Fourth of July was one of the big holidays of the year for all comunities in the state, and Milpitas wasn't left out. Rathbone's store in 1859 was decked out in flags and had a cannon "on the piazza" that was fired off at sunrise, noon and sunset, according to Doten.

Chapter II

The decade of the '60s was marked by war.

The long and bitter battle between the incoming settlers and the owners of the huge land grants exploded the length of Santa Clara Valley, and the outbreak of the faraway Civil War brought heated encounters between Union and Confederate sympathizers.

The land battle was born of faulty titles and surveys, of greedy lawyers and land speculators, and out of the language difficulties between the Spanish-speaking owners and the gringo.

Rancho Milpitas was the center of a bitter controversy, not only involving the newcomers who wanted to carve farms out of its rich acres, but because of the antagonism that had grown between two families who claimed the same land grant.

Rancho Milpitas had been granted originally to Nicolas Berryessa by an alcalde of San Jose who mistakenly believed he had the power to parcel out land grants. The following year, 1835, Governor Jose Castro, acting with more legal authority, granted the same hunk of land to Jose Maria Alviso.

It wasn't until 1871 that the U.S. Land Commission confirmed title to the Alviso family, and by that time both Nicolas Berryessa and Jose Maria Alviso were dead.

The early part of the decade hovered on the verge of a shooting war which failed to break out, although fences were cut, houses burned, cattle allowed to run loose and destroy crops.

Rates of Toll

ON THE SAN JOSE AND ALVISO

TURNPIKE ROAD!

All the way from San Jose to Alviso, or from Alviso to San Jose:

Loaded Wagons, drawn by Two horses, oxen or mules,				- - -	$1 0_
" " " Four " "				- - -	1 5_
" " " Six " "				- - -	2 00
Empty Wagons, one-half the above rates.					
Every additional horse in team,			- - - - -	12½
Stages, Omnibusses, and other vehicles carrying freight or passengers, same as Wagons.					
One horse Buggy or Carriage,			- - - - - - -	37½
Two " " "			- - - - - - -	50
Single Horse with rider,			. . . .	25
Loose Horses, any number less than ten, each,			. . .	5
Ten, or more than ten, for each ten and the fraction over,			. .	40
Single Cow, with or without sucking calf,			. . . .	5
Loose Cattle, more than one and less than ten, each,			. . .	4
Ten or more, for each ten and the fraction over,			. . .	30
Single Sheep or Hog,			. . . .	5
More than one and less than ten, each,			. . . .	3
Ten or more than ten, for each ten and the fraction over,			. .	25

☞ Any animals not enumerated above, at the same rates. ☜

From May 14th to October 14th, inclusive, half the above rates.

Wagons or Carts having wheels with more than 2½ inches tread, the toll to be reduced at the rate of 12½ per cent. for every ¼ inch over 2½ inches.

Between the Milpitas road and Alviso, one-eighth the above rates.

Between the Milpitas road and San Jose, three-fourths the above rates.

Between the Milpitas road and Lick's Mill, one-fourth the above rates.

Between the road at Lick's Mill and either Alviso or San Jose, one-half the full rates first above named.

WM. DANIELS, President S. J. & A. T. R. Co.

The Law Regulating Tolls and Toll Gates.

Sec. 29. Each toll-gatherer may detain and prevent from passing through his gate, the persons leading or driving animals or carriages subject to toll, until they shall have paid respectively the tolls authorized by law.

Sec. 31. Every toll-gatherer who, at any gate, shall unreasonable hinder or delay any traveler or passenger liable to the payment of toll, or shall demand and receive from any person more than by law he is authorized to collect, shall, for each offence, forfeit the sum of $10 to the person aggrieved.

Sec. 33. Every person who, to avoid the payment of the legal toll, shall, with his team, carriage or horse, turn out of a turnpike road or plank road, or pass any gate thereon on ground adjacent thereto, and again enter upon such road, shall, for each offence, forfeit the sum of _ _ to the corporation injured.—Wood's Digest.

Owen & Cottle, Printers, San Jose Mercury.

Former Milpitan William Daniels was president of this toll road 1861-63.

14

The settlers, some who had squatted on what they believed was government land and some who had paid the land owners only to find other claimants to the same land, organized to raise funds to fight for their farms. The sheriff was busy trying to serve eviction notices and making them stick.

It was a heyday for the lawyers, many of whom were out to make a fortune for themselves. They were not above fast-talking some of the Mexican and Spanish landowners out of large chunks of their property because the latter did not understand the language or the law. Land was often given in lieu of cash for lawyers' fees. The great ranchos dwindled in size but only the lawyers got rich.

Doten lost his land in the dispute over the southern boundary of Rancho Milpitas during the unsettled time of the land title battles, and his diary mentions several instances of interest.

In 1860 he notes the sheriff came to move the Berryessa family out of their house and asked Doten and others to help, which they refused. The sheriff was acting on a complaint of Jose Urridias, who had married the widow of Jose Maria Alviso and was managing the Alviso rancho affairs.

Bart Sepulveda, descendant of the Alviso family, said Urridias was selling off parcels of the Alviso grant as needed. The children of Juana Alviso Urridias were not happy with the situation and demanded their share of their father's estate. They claimed the land could not be sold by Urridias because they were the rightful heirs.

"The death of Urridias in 1869 further complicated the matter," according to Sepulveda, and "through the years of law suits and countersuits no one benefitted except the courts, the government and the lawyers." These fees took a great bulk of the estate.

"When Juana Galindo de Urridias died in 1885 the Probate Court divided what was left of the rancho among

María de los Ángeles Alviso (1843-1918) m. Bartolome Sepulveda. Bart Sepulveda photo.

16

the heirs, who for one reason or another sold their shares to outsiders."

Sepulveda said the only part remaining still in the hands of descendants at the time of this writing is a portion homesteaded by Urridias in 1857 and left directly to Jose Maria's youngest daughter, Maria Guadalupe de los Angles Alviso Sepulveda. This property, known as part of lot 18, was deeded to "Angela" Sepulveda and her husband Bartolo Sepulveda, when she became 21 years of age in 1865. This is the property still farmed by her grandson, John Morgan Sepulveda (Bart's father) across Piedmont Boulevard from the old Jose Maria Alviso adobe.

In Doten's time Urridias was claiming grazing rights on the south side of Berryessa Creek, which was later proved not to be in the Alviso grant, and on which both the Berryessa family and Doten were living.

The sheriff moved the furniture out of the Berryessa house and the family moved it back. Then the sheriff came and evicted the Berryessas again, this time boarding up the house.

Doten bought land from Abram Harris who owned part of Agua Caliente. Doten pulled up some of his fence posts and trees and, in the dead of night, hauled about everything that wasn't nailed down to his new place in defiance of Urridias. He finally burned the house, for which Urridias got the blame from the frustrated settlers.

The U.S. Land Commission confirmed title to Agua Caliente Rancho in 1858, and issued a patent on Rancho Tularcitos to the Jose Higuera heirs in 1870.

Although land title problems continued, the Civil War stirred up other situations not always peaceful.

News of the fall of Fort Sumpter reached California by Pony Express April 25, 1861, and on May 11 a mass meeting was held in San Francisco at which support for the Union was pledged.

Adobe home of Josepha Castro (eldest daughter of Jose Maria Alviso) east side of Piedmont Road 100 feet north of Uridias Ranch Road. Florence Lee (Ogier) Hawley photo.

Thousands of Southerners had come West during the gold rush to settle in the Golden State. Many of these kept their Southern sympathies and were active, especially in the San Joaquin Valley and Southern California, in schemes to cripple the state's support of the Union and to aid the Confederacy.

However, Union sympathizers were in the majority and some 15,000 volunteers enlisted to fight for the Union, although few ever saw active service. California led the nation in contributions to the Sanitary Commission (forerunner of the Red Cross), sending nearly a million dollars to aid the sick and wounded in the far away war. Doten noted October 12, 1862 that $200 had been collected at Creighton's store in Milpitas for the Union Sanitary Fund.

Towns and cities formed home guard units. Five companies known as the California Battalion went east and joined a Massachusetts regiment, and eight companies were recruited in San Francisco for the First Washington Regiment. Other companies were formed to go to New Mexico, Kansas, Arizona, Oregon and Utah to protect the overland mail route and emigrant trains against Indian attack.

Milpitas did not have a home guard, but several of its young men undoubtedly joined up with the Alviso Rifles, commanded by Thatcher F. Barnes, who had a farm between Alviso and Milpitas.

However, as with the majority of Californians, most Milpitans were unaffected by the Civil War during its duration.

Doten notes the war was felt by "way of missing friends, rising prices and increased taxation." Congress had levied the first U.S. income tax in 1861 to raise funds for the Union forces.

Political rallies were numerous in the early 1860's, and fights between the Union faction and the Jeff Davis men were frequent. Election Day was an occasion when all the men folks went to town to vote and get in a last word for their candidate over a few glasses of whiskey at Rathbone's, which was the polling place in Milpitas. In the election in 1861 Rathbone raised a flag pole over 100 feet high in front of his place and there was drum and fife music and a few speeches, according to Doten's diary.

He describes the July 4, 1862 celebration held in Mountain View, with a huge picnic, speeches, and the dance in the evening. Many Milpitans and Berryessa people were on hand for the festivities, including "the three Misses Evans, Miss Annie Wiseheart, Cal Taylor (who) brought a big load of the Berryessa boys, Jim Johnson, Charley Fowler and the Berryessa cannon." He notes they brought a banner "Settlers rights and Union forever."

It was a political rally in 1863 that spawned a saying that old timers were to chuckle over for decades. The rally was held in San Jose and the speaker was the famed Unitarian preacher, Thomas Starr King, whose "matchless oratory saved California for the Union." A number of loyal Unionists from Milpitas showed up with a banner reading: "As goes Milpitas, so goes the State."

The slogan was quoted up and down California and the San Jose Mercury, dated September 14, 1880 ran a long, rambling article attempting to explain another obscure reference to "the man from Milpitas" who allegedly was being quoted on all manner of issues and in all parts of the nation.

The "As Goes Milpitas" saying at this time probably did as much to poke fun at the little community as vaudeville did a few decades later.

One of the violent acts that came pretty close to home during the Civil War years was the burning of the Methodist Church in Berryessa, allegedly by members of the notorious Dick Baker gang of Confederates.

This was one of several companies organized to raise money for the Confederate cause mainly by robbing stages and banks.

French's Hotel burned January 17, 1861, but was immediately rebuilt and a grand ball held on the opening June 6. Doten in his diary notes some 200 attended the party, including some 50 ladies, "among whom were several very good looking Spanish girls."

This notation points up the fact that in those times it was really "a man's world." The great migration to California had brought mainly young men, or those who left families behind until they could make a home for them in the new land.

Doten said that tickets to the ball were $5 and the dance lasted until 7 a.m. the next day. There were two bands for music and dancing was in the hall above and the parlor below. It took three hours to serve the midnight supper due to lack of table accommodations.

There was a lot doing in Milpitas in 1861, much of it social. On May Day there was a picnic in Calaveras Valley attended by most Milpitans, followed by a dance in Sherman's big barn that lasted until 5 a.m.

Another picnic was held in the Calaveras Valley July 4, with a ball that night in French's Hotel.

Floods late in March destroyed much of the planted grain. The Coyote Creek went over its banks and "a small house floated off," Doten writes. North of town much of the land was under water, "chickens on top of the house, pigs swimming, a man rescued from a haystack with a boat" and there was no stage for several days.

The same thing happened in December and there was no stage to Oakland for a week. The rains continued into January, 1862 and the whole country around Milpitas and San Jose was a sheet of water. The Sacramento and San Joaquin Valleys were wall-to-wall water. Boats were used in the streets of Sacramento and in Alameda County around Alvarado and Union City.

The following year drought struck California and stockmen around Milpitas lost many cattle and horses.

Capt. Calvin Valpey home at Harrisburg (Warm Springs) 1876.

22

By 1861 Milpitas Township was formed, bounded by Coyote Creek, Alameda County, Stanislaus County and Berryessa Creek. O.H.P. Vennum, Berryessa farmer, was the first justice of the peace and J.W. Johnson the first constable.

Others who served as justices during the 1860s were Wilson Brown, Marshall Pomeroy, D.K. Fuller and Alfred French. Constables of the period were William Gaines, M. McStay and J.J. Schemmerhorn.

Pioneers of the 1860s included Englishmen William Jacklin, John Winsor and Samuel Ayer, 49er Matthew Dixon, Nova Scotia sea captain Calvin Valpey, Ireland-born Michael Bellew, Canadians Joseph Bradshaw, Edward Topham and David Boyce, New Yorker Reuben Barber, Missourian William J. Burnett, Charles Beverson from Germany and Henry Curtner from Indiana.

Valpey, who was to give his name to a mountain ridge and a creek far east of Milpitas in the Diablo range, had come to San Francisco in 1851, and had operated schooners on the bay for several years before sending for his family and buying property at Harrisburg.

Dixon was a neighbor of the Valpey family, coming to Harrisburg and buying land on both sides of the county line in 1861 after a brief go at mining in the Placerville area.

He built his house back from the Mission Road and constructed a lane from there to his landing and warehouses near the side of the much later Fremont Airport. Valpey built a landing next to Dixon's.

Two-masted schooners and flat-bottomed scows tied up at the crude docks to load hay, grain and produce from Milpitas and Southern Alameda County.

The two-story Dixon house was shaken off its foundation in the October, 1868 earthquake and Mrs. Dixon was pinned by her long skirts between the porch and the wall of the house until rescued by her young son.

The building was later moved to south Main Street (the name given Mission Road through the Milpitas business district) adjacent to St. John the Baptist Catholic Church and became the residence of the Henry Abel family for many years.

The first school in Harrisburg opened in 1863 on the property of John Wilson south of the Warm Springs landing operated by the Baker brothers (land which became part of the Curtner holdings). Wilson later became a state assemblyman.

Lizzie Valpey (later Mrs. Henry Shaw) was the first teacher in the one-room school. She was the daughter of Capt. Valpey and was "sparked" by Alfred Doten for a few months before he left Milpitas to go to the silver mines of Nevada in 1863.

Jacklin had come "around the horn" to San Francisco in 1859, and the following year was running cattle in the hills east of Milpitas. It was in 1878 he bought the 185-acre Marshall Pomeroy ranch east of Mission Road and north of Milpitas, the area later marked by Jacklin Road.

Pomeroy was a native of Connecticut who came to California in 1858 via the Isthmus. He went to the mines for several years before coming to Milpitas where in 1867 he married Ella French, daughter of the hotelkeeper.

Winsor almost didn't get to Milpitas. Coming overland in 1852, he became ill and was left beside the wagon trail in Utah Territory to die. Nursed back to health by Indians, he spent the winter trapping and then joined another California-bound train.

At the mines on the American River, Winsor met a man newly arrived from his hometown in Iowa who told him his wife had learned of his death and had remarried.

Winsor gave up mining in 1856 and after working a while on a farm in the San Joaquin Valley, came to Mission San Jose where he met and (in 1858) married an Irish girl named Catherine Costello. For about five years the Winsors lived back in the hills in the Smith Creek area, then came to Milpitas and bought 40 acres on the Milpitas-Berryessa Road (now Capitol Avenue).

Samuel Ayer was 20 years old when he came to California via the Isthmus of Panama in 1860. In Milpitas he first worked for the Wellers, and then set up his own blacksmith business. In 1868 he leased the shop and went into ranching, buying 150 acres a mile east of town. He married America Evans, daughter of neighbor Josiah Evans, in 1862.

Michael Bellew was another ex-gold miner who wound up farming and operating a dairy in Milpitas in the 1860s. He came to California by the sea route in 1853 and before coming to Milpitas in the summer of 1861 worked for the government at Mare island. His farm was west of town on the Alviso-Milpitas Road.

Charles Beverson came to the area in 1868 and built his home place on the Mission Road south of Milpitas. He operated an 86-acre dairy in Laguna Valley for a time, and had a 2,000 acre cattle ranch 23 miles back in the hills near Valpey's place.

Bradshaw arrived about mid-decade and bought land in Laguna Valley and up off what became Felter Road.

Boyce had gone to the mines and then followed the blacksmith trade in Redwood City and over on the coast in Spanishtown (Half Moon Bay) before coming to Milpitas and going to Sam Ayer's shop in 1867. He had just built his own shop when fellow Canadian Topham arrived to join him.

The shop with its sign "Boyce & Topham" high up on the false-fronted building was a landmark on Main Street into the 20th century.

Curtner, who had been a farmer and steamboat captain, took passage to San Francisco from New York in 1852 and arrived nearly penniless. He found work on farms around Mission San Jose, returned to Indiana in 1856 to marry and bring his bride to a 50-acre farm he bought near Alvarado. In the late 1860's he bought the first of the thousands of acres of Rancho Tularcitos he would own on the Alameda-Santa Clara county line.

Samuel Ayer home on north side of Calaveras Road (later site of Big Yellow House restaurant). Florence Lee (Ogier) Hawley photo.

Barber had come to California in 1852 and was farming in the Milpitas area in the 1860s, but returned east for 14 years and didn't settle permanently on his land west of town until 1880.

Burnett was 10 years old when his family left Missouri for the Santa Clara Valley, the overland trip consuming two years. His father died when the wagon train reached Stockton and young William found himself the head of the household. The family farmed at Mountain View until moving to Milpitas in 1867 and buying 170 acres east of the Evans place.

Doten attended the grand opening of George W. Peacock's saloon and hotel at Harrisburg July 20, 1862, and the wedding of Clymena French and Samuel Shearer at French's Hotel. (The Shearer family later joined other ranchers raising cattle back in the remote country east of the Arroyo Honda.)

There was much excitement throughout Santa Clara County in the early 1860s with discovery of outcroppings of gold, silver, copper and other minerals near Gilroy, in Alum Rock canyon, and in the western mountains.

Doten reported in his diary of January 7, 1863 that gold had been discovered "at the head of Calaveras Valley" by an old man named Miller.

With more and more settlers crowding into Calaveras and Laguna Valleys there was a need for more schools.

Sam Sherman gave a piece of land and the Calaveras School District came into being August 6, 1862. Sherman served a number of years as trustee and clerk of the board, and other early trustees included Dudley Wells, John Patton, John Carrick and John G. Messersmith.

During the decade two other schools were added in the hill country, Mission Peak, high on the mountain above Joseph Weller's ranch, and Laguna, near the gap in the hills where the road ran down into Calaveras Valley.

Mission Peak lasted only briefly, closing in 1865 when John W. Braden and A.D.Smith were trustees. Laguna was formed February 17, 1865, with trustees J.S. Dooley, Hiram Pomeroy, and W.S. Gaines.

Laguna School, which was to continue until the 1940s, was only in session six months the first year or so. The teacher was paid $60 a month, including board.

In Milpitas, the grammar school began receiving state funds and the Milpitas School District was formed Febuary 7, 1860, according to county school records.

The 1856 school was enlarged in 1868 by an addition of 33 x 40 feet.

The *San Jose Mercury* in May, 1866, reported on the financial condition of the county schools, most of which were in good shape, but Laguna School was $3.89 in the red.

There was excitement in Milpitas Sept. 6, 1869 when the first train came chugging through town from Sacramento. This was the Western Pacific (later the Southern Pacific) and the line was built via Stockton to San Jose. Earlier in the year, the transcontinental railroad had been completed with ceremonies at Promontory Point in Utah Territory.

In October, 1869, a disastrous fire swept through Calaveras Valley starting at the head of the valley near County Supervisor David Campbell's place and burning over many acres of the Sherman, Merritt and Buick ranches. Consumed in the fast-moving blaze which neighbors fought all night, were hundreds of bales of hay and sacks of grain, as well as 60 cords of wood and much fencing.

One of the first railroad accidents in the area occurred in mid-October, 1869, on the month-old Western Pacific Railroad at the crossing on the Milpitas road. The *San Jose Mercury* reported "Mr. Fleming was returning from Alviso hauling a load of grain with a double team." The dust obscured his vision and the lead horses had crossed the track when he heard the whistle. He was injured and three horses were killed.

By the end of the decade the population of Milpitas Township was 645.

Chapter III

Agriculture was coming into its own in the Milpitas area in the 1870s.

Vegetables were being grown in the warm belt along the foothills, vineyards and orchards were coming into being, and hay and grain fields were wiping out the miles of waving mustard that once marked the flatlands.

Also disappearing were the huge old oaks on the valley floor, and in the draws and canyons of the hill country, mostly cut for firewood. Elk and antelope and grizzly bear were practically all gone, but mountain lions and coyotes still roamed the hills, and great flocks of geese and ducks still swept in from the bay in the fall when the cottonwoods along the creek turned yellow.

Deer were plentiful and ranchers complained they were regularly getting braver, coming down out of the hills to sample the grain and grapes.

Fishing was good in the streams, and John E. Haley in 1874 told the San Jose *Mercury* of a 20-inch, three-pound brook trout hooked "near the Hog Ranch" on Calaveras Creek.

Some pesky varmints had increased to plague the farmer. Gophers and ground squirrels were a big problem and county supervisors formed squirrel and gopher districts which carried a one-cent tax per resident.

This tax was on top of the poll tax, road taxes, school fund and infirmary fund, and railroad taxes assessed by the county. There was even a dollar tax on all dogs.

Game laws were enacted in 1874, setting seasons for trout fishing, the hunting of elk, quail and dove, and making it illegal to use dogs in the hunting of deer, snares in the hunting of quail, or nets or wire-baskets in the taking of trout.

Milpitas Township was getting almost crowded, according to the folks who remembered the countryside a couple of decades back. The roofs of barns and houses were now a part of the landscape in all directions as viewed from the growing town.

Roads were being widened and surfaced to handle the heavy wagon traffic as farmers hauled their produce to the railroad or the various landings on the bay.

Social events still included rodeos and July 4 celebrations, picnics, dances at French's Hotel and an occasional horse race. There were also traveling medicine shows, camp meetings, political gatherings in the schoolhouse, and church affairs.

Although there was no local newspaper, Milpitans read in San Francisco and San Jose papers of happenings elsewhere during the decade of the '70s. . . the manufacture of barbed wire, founding of the Women's Christian Temperance Union, the invention of the telephone and the electric light, and production of the first commercial milking machine.

They rode San Francisco's first cable cars, and the narrow gauge railroad over the mountains to Santa Cruz.

Milpitans were among the several thousand attending the big party in celebration of the victory of Berryessa settlers in their 20-year battle for title to their lands.

The settlers had bought the lands of the City of San Jose believing the Berryessa family had no grant and that the territory was public land. The Berryessa claim had been rejected by the courts but Oakland attorney Horace Carpentier had gotten hold of most of the land.

His claim was finally proved fraudulent and the Supreme Court confirmed titles to the settlers, giving a grand excuse for a mammoth feast, complete with congratulatory speeches and a dance in the Berryessa schoolhouse.

Milpitas residents were in the crowd that turned out for the hanging of bandit Tiburcio Vasquez in the San Jose jail yard March 19, 1875.

Some of the oldtimers the following year attended the funeral of San Jose City Clerk Montgomery Maze, former Pony Express rider who had married the daughter of Harrisburg pioneer, Joseph Scott.

Milpitas watched with interest the construction of the Lick Road up Mt. Hamilton and no doubt chuckled over the humorous article in the San Jose *Mercury* relating to the trip up the road made by county supervisors, including Milpitas' own Samuel Ayer, Jan. 9, 1877.

The anonymous reporter couldn't resist poking fun at Milpitas (or at Ayer) and wrote how the supervisor described the view as the carriage climbed high above the valley.

"His face glowing with pride. . . his voice swelling with patriotism," Supervisor Ayer pointed out San Jose and Santa Clara and waved his arm in the direction of Milpitas.

"But his look of exultation changed to disappointment, disgust and indignation, and he exclaimed: 'If some durned fool hadn't gone and built a barn in the valley and shut Milpitas out of sight!' "

The 1870s marked the arrival in Milpitas Township of the first of the many Portuguese farmers who would help make the area one of Santa Clara County's richest truck garden and row crop sections.

From the Azores Islands came Antonio Joseph, who had first farmed in San Mateo County where he was naturalized in 1870, and Joseph Pedro, who took out citizenship papers in San Jose in 1887.

Alexander deRose Coelho, a native of Portugal, stopped off in Boston where he became a U.S. citizen in 1872 before coming to Mipitas.

The decade also brought Elhanan W. Darling and the Whealan (also spelled Whalen) family from Canada, blacksmith Henry W. Wigmore from England, Charles H. Cropley from Nova Scotia, wagonmaker Carl F. Olinder from Sweden, New Yorkers Mandeville and Marshall Pixley, and Alfred Felter, who gave his name to the winding road that went past his mountain ranch.

Others included Vermont harnessmaker Alfred Jones, butchers W.D. Castle from Michigan and Henry Abel from Wisconsin; Pennsylvanian William Murphy who married the widow Mary Shaughnessy whose farm was along the Coyote south of the Alviso-Milpitas Road.

John C. Dempsey and Thomas Russell came from Ireland to farm and leave their names on Milpitas roads.

Russell's neighbors up off the Mission Road north of town chuckled over his first encounter with the fine points of hitching up a team. Russell had spent his early life as a seaman and was much more familiar with a ship's rigging than that of a team of horses. The first time he unhitched his team he took the harness apart.

Perhaps the most significant happening in Milpitas Township in the 1870s, and one that was to affect a large segment of the mountain population years later, was the announced plan of a San Francisco water company to dam Calaveras Valley.

The San Jose *Mercury,* April 29, 1874, indicated there was little hope for the valley agriculturally because "a company has been organized in San Francisco for the purpose of buying the land and erecting a dam across the valley where it joins Sunol, to transform the whole thing into an immense reservoir to supply San Francisco with water."

The announcement caused concern among the more than 60 farmers in the valley, some of whom decided to accept the inevitable and sold to the firm which became known as Spring Valley Water Co. Others sold and then rented their land back from the company, continuing to farm for many years.

A San Jose *Mercury* reporter sent out into the countryside to assess the crops and agricultural progress in April, 1874, mentions one of those concerned was Nick Harris. Hiram Pomeroy and Dudley Wells were among those who sold to the company in 1875.

Because the *Mercury* reporter's tour is of interest to this history of the 1870s, we decided to follow along.

Coming out the Mission Road from San Jose, the first stop was at the farm of James Murphy where it was found worms were causing extensive damage to Murphy's wheat.

Skirting the town of Milpitas, the reporter visited the Samuel Ayer place of 150 acres lying about midway between the town and the foothills. Ayer had 100 acres in wheat and the rest in grass.

At the foothills, J.M. Janes' farm of 155 acres was planted to hay.

"He has some fine young stock," the reporter writes, "including a Messenger and a Hambletonian colt, and has completed his new two-story home.

"Taking the road through the Laguna to Calaveras Valley we found the grain looking splendidly, and all the farmers concurring in the opinion the crop prospects the best ever known in the county.

"Mrs. Mary Miller's place, located on the right of the road near the Laguna, has 110 acres of which 50 are in barley and about 40 in wheat. The place is farmed by her two sons who are making preparations for thorough experimenting with alfalfa next season," the reporter continues.

"Alex Anderson has let his ranch out on shares, part to some Italians who are raising vegetables and part to some Portuguese who are raising grain. Both crops are doing well. . . the vegetables are being grown on the hills, which seem to be specially adapted to this. . .

"Just above Mrs. Miller's place is the Laguna shop presided over by Joseph Bradshaw who does the manufacturing and repairing of implements, wagons, etc., for the country for miles around. He has all he can do and does it well.

"Thos. Harrison's place is situated just above the Laguna School house, and comprises 600 acres... of wheat, hay and pasture. Everything about Mr. Harrison's place betokens the careful farmer... a neat picket fence surrounds his dooryard, in which he has planted a large number of choice plants and flowers... a couple of young orange trees... a number of Monterey cypresses... a vegetable garden without a weed to be seen in it.

"About a mile from the school house we come to the Calaveras Valley, one of the beauty spots of the world.

"The first place we visited on entering the valley was John Sherman's. He has 400 acres lying on the west side of the valley, of which 200 acres is in wheat, 10 acres in barley, 18 acres in flax and the rest in hay. The flax is an experiment and very likely to succeed... now about 8 inches high.

"Ex-County Supervisor David Campbell's place adjoins Sherman's," the reporter continues. He has 200 acres also planted to wheat, barley and flax, and has a contract with the Oil and Lead Works of San Francisco to take his flax seed at $2.25 per hundred pounds.

"Ex-sheriff (Nick) Harris lives in clover on his 200-acre tract adjoining Campbell. He has his place all in wheat except about 10 acres in barley.

"Nick is one of the pioneers of the Calaveras, he and Dudley Wells, Campbell, Brown and Rix all coming in and taking up land together. They packed in their implements and seed on horses and started what are now the prettiest farms in this state," the reporter wrote.

"The first white woman in the valley was Mrs. Vesey, who came in with her husband sometime after (Harris and others). The news of her advent spread far and wide and created as great a sensation as Cortez did among the Mexicans."

34

(Author's note: Mrs. Vesey was the wife of J.M. Vesey, friend of diarist Alfred Doten when he lived at Harrisburg, and later when Vesey had a hotel at Gold Hill, Nev.)

"Next to Harris, Hiram Pomeroy has 170 acres, 90 of which is planted to grain. He also raises bees, chickens, milks nine cows, and has an orchard and small vineyard," according to the reporter, who adds "Pomeroy sells eggs, wine and butter.

"W.S. Gaines has 200 acres of valley land and 575 acres in the hills. The flat land is planted to wheat and Gaines is planning to sow 20 acres of alfalfa next season. Dudley Wells' farm of over 200 acres adjoins Gaines', mostly in wheat, but 20 acres is in potatoes.

"Wells has a beautiful home surrounded by fine trees. . . He is roadmaster of that district and is making and repairing the highways on the same principle that he farms his land: thoroughly and well."

John Carrick was growing wheat on the southeast edge of the valley and experimenting with growing alfalfa on the dry hillside for pasturing his stock. Here the reporter notes that, while wheat is the principle crop in the Calaveras, "every farmer has his orchard or vineyard or both, and all the valley surroundings indicate that the people are working for a home as well as for money."

Returning to Milpitas, the reporter visited the Josiah Evans ranch, located partly in the hills and partly in the valley.

"His house, which he expects soon to be replaced by a new one, stands on the first rise of the hills commanding a fine view of the valley and surrounding country. He has a fine orchard of different varieties of fruits together with a number of walnut and almond trees."

He also mentions the Evans place is in the warm belt and Evans is planning to set out a number of orange trees next season as an experiment.

The reporter visited the M.W. Dixon ranch, 600 acres

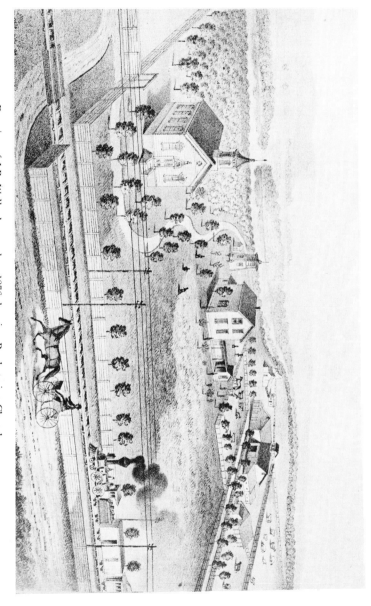

Drawing of J.R. Weller home place 1876 showing Presbyterian Church.

on the Warm Springs road and partly in Alameda County. It was pointed out an effort was made at the last Legislative session to change the county boundaries which would bring the entire Dixon ranch into Santa Clara County, but it failed. One of the features of the ranch is the Warm Springs landing belonging to Dixon and Capt. Valpey, the reporter noted.

J.R. Weller had 197 acres of valley land and about 300 in the hills northeast of Milpitas, mostly devoted to hay and pasture. He had a dairy and his butter "is much sought after." It was also noted Weller had just built a new home.

A large quantity of land in and around Milpitas was rented, and the crops are looking well, the writer notes before exploring the town of Milpitas in which he mentions the school under the supervision of Miss Palmer, which had an average attendance of about 65 pupils.

"A beautiful church has just been completed under the auspices of the Presbyterian congregation, which adds materially to the appearance of the town.

"Topham's wagon and agricultural implement factory is crowded with work...Olinder's blacksmithing establishment has all it can do to fill its orders...Jones' harness shop and Barthel's boot and shoe shop are turning out good work and meeting with a liberal patronage."

The *Mercury* reporter concludes the Milpitas area tour with the following comments:

"A large number of new dwellings have been erected during the year in Milpitas and the numerous improvements on every side testify to an era of prosperity.

"At the junction of the Alviso and Milpitas road with the Coyote, the water has backed up and formed a dangerous mudhole, which will long be remembered by all who have had occasion to pass that way. We are glad to be able to state that under the superintendency of the efficient roadmaster Dudley Wells, rocks are being hauled from the hills and a roadbed built across the slough.''

The Pioneer Society of Santa Clara County was organized in 1875 and among charter members from the Milpitas area were Dudley Wells and John Trimble.

Samuel Ayer became the first supervisor of the newly formed Milpitas district in 1875.

Nick Harris served as sheriff of the county from 1870 to 1872 and again from 1876 to the end of the decade.

Joseph R. Weller was elected a delegate to the State Constitutional Convention in 1878.

Serving as Justices of the Peace in the 1870s were J.R. Weller, Alfred French, Michael Barthel, a Frenchman who later was a San Jose shoemaker, and Edward Topham. Constables included one of the Pixleys, John Sherman, Marshall Pomeroy and J.J. Schemmerhorn.

Chapter IV

During the decade of the '80s strawberries and asparagus became major crops and the town of Milpitas, with an estimated 200 citizens, became an important supply and shipping center.

Although not directly involved, Milpitas was touched by events of the decade such as the Chinese immigration question, which threatened the labor force needed for the strawberry industry.

Ninety per cent of the strawberries for the San Francisco market were grown in Milpitas, Alviso, Agnew and The Willows (Willow Glen), and the Chinese controlled the industry.

Kenneth Chow, writing in the book "Chinese Argonauts," says "anybody who wanted to go into the business of growing strawberries must consult the 'Chinaman'."

The white landowner wishing to raise strawberries, but realizing the difficulties in getting his countrymen for the "stoop labor" required, leased or sharecropped his land to the Chinese who planted, cultivated and harvested the crop.

The Chinese decided how many acres to plant. If the lessee felt an increase in production would flood the market, the landowners did not get an increase in acres. Or if he planted too many, there would be no Chinese in the fields to pick the berries at harvest time.

Up until 1850 only a few Chinese had come to California, but with the gold rush and the building of the railroads, their numbers increased until by the 1880s there were some 120,000 in the state.

Most were common laborers brought into California by wealthy Chinese organizations known as the Six Companies. The laborers were under contract to the organizations, promising to pay back their passage to this country and to turn over a percentage of their earnings. In return, the companies guaranteed the laborers jobs and promised to get them back to China.

The Chinese in California kept to themselves, declining to adopt the white man's customs or manner of life. They were often persecuted and resented by labor because of their willingness to work cheap.

"The Californian," writes Robert Glass Cleland in his "History of California, the American Period," "saw in the Chinaman only an inferior being, simple in some ways, but cannier than a Scot in others, who lived in squalor and stench, spoke an outlandish jargon, worked with a patience and industry beyond comprehension, worshipped strange gods, suffered from strange diseases, practiced strange vices, ate strange foods, regarded China as the land of the blessed, thrived under standards of living no white man could endure, administered his own law in his own way through his own agents without much regard for the officials and statutes of the Sovereign State of California, (and) suffered with helpless stoicism whatever indignities were thrust upon him..."

By the 1880s there was strong talk that "the Chinese must go," and many influential men in the state and the county were listed on the rolls of the Anti-Coolie League.

The 1880s were marked by such national events as the assassination of President Garfield, the death of Billy the Kid and the horror of the Johnstown flood, all of which

40

were topics of discussion in Pixley's saloon or around the potbellied stove in Philander Clark's general store on Main Street in Milpitas.

Pea growers in the area read with interest of the invention of a machine to separate pea pods from the vines, and several farmers were experimenting with a new berry named for its Santa Cruz founder, Judge James Logan.

By the 1880s, the old Mission Road was being called the Oakland Road, and Harrisburg had taken the name of Warm Springs.

James Boyd, a newcomer to the area, bought the O'Toole place south of town. A year later, in 1883, he sold it to Santa Clara County for an almshouse.

The property, containing 100 acres with barns and a three-story, 20-room mansion John O'Toole had built for his family in the 1860s, was purchased by the county for $25,000, a sum the Grand Jury argued was too much to pay.

The mansion was dubbed "a poorhouse in a palace" and one James Finley was hired as superintendent to operate the dairy, chicken and hog enterprises, manage the vegetable and fruit growing, as well as the hay and grain crops, all of which were to supply food for the County Infirmary, jail and the Almshouse.

Major businesses in Milpitas in the 1880s included N.M. Pixley's saloon and boarding house, the latter competing somewhat with Alfred French, who still ran the hotel and who also served during the decade as justice of the peace of Milpitas Township. Other Main Street businesses included Olinder's blacksmith and wagon shop, Clark's store, Abel's butcher business, Alex Wigmore's boot and shoe shop, and Alfred Jones' harness and saddle store.

A.F. Cunha had a saloon and general store, and also served as postmaster.

Henry Topham and Charley Cropley teamed up in the grain-buying business and built a 350 by 40-foot warehouse

Hay baling crew 1886. Clyde Arbuckle photo.

42

to accommodate growers who did not wish to ship their grain immediately after harvest. E.W.Darling also built a warehouse which held 4,000 tons of grain.

Edward Topham and David Boyce were advertising the "well-known Milpitas fruit wagon" and the manufacture of the "Milpitas Harrow" in their shop. They were also selling the new fencing material called "barbed wire," or, by some, "Devil's rope."

Nineteen-year-old Aldace N. Ashley came to Milpitas with his family in 1883, his dad going into partnership with James K.P. Dixon to operate a general store, in which young Aldace worked until buying the partners out in 1887. But more importantly for Milpitas, by this year Ashley was agent for the Sunset Telephone Co., the firm founded a few years earlier in San Jose and now reaching out for customers in the surrounding communities.

Shoppers at Ashley's or Clark's stores in the mid'1880s were paying $1.50 for 50 pounds of flour, 10 cents a can for oysters, 25 cents for a dozen eggs, the same for a dozen candles, 40 cents for a broom and 50 cents for a lamp chimney.

Winter rains caused the usual problems, but no major flooding occurred except in March 1884, when storms turned much of the road west of town into a lake, and washed out railroad tracks north of the Alameda County line.

Helping to swell the population of the 1880s were several men of Portuguese descent whose families would become prominent in area agriculture and in the life of the town. These included Jose A. Simas of Portugal who opened a barbershop (his son, Joe, would become the town's historian some 60 years later), Antone J. Spangler, also from Portugal, Domingos A. Silva, John R. Carlo, J.F. Serpa, and Frank Terra, all from the Azores Islands.

Benjamin Gordon family at their home on Calaveras Road 1890s. Clyde Arbuckle photo.

Spangler was a farmer, but his son, Anthony, later opened a garage in Milpitas. Carlo was a youngster when he arrived, and he attended school at Warm Springs and later farmed part of the Curtner ranch on Downing Road before becoming a Milpitas merchant.

Silva ranched on Piedmont Road east of town, and Serpa farmed in Laguna Valley.

Terra was to operate a blacksmith and farm machinery manufacturing business in Milpitas for more than 40 years.

The William F. Downing family came over from Nevada in 1881 and bought land east of the Evans place and north of Laguna Valley where Downing Road was later cut into Calaveras Road. The ranch was purchased from Henry Curtner and was part of Ranchos Tularcitos and Agua Caliente.

One of the first to rent land from the Downings was another Silva, Joseph, who came to the area in 1886, and whose family continued to farm the land half-way through the 20th century.

Also arriving in the 1880s were the Trousdell brothers, Joseph W., Henry John, and Charles, who were born in the mining country near Jackson, and who were stockmen.

About this time Benjamin H. Gordon, pioneer of 1846 and grandfather of San Jose historian Clyde Arbuckle, settled with his family in Laguna Valley. Teenager James Hansen came from Denmark to work on the ranch of his uncle, Lawrence Martin Hansen, and attend Laguna School with the children of the Arbuckle, Miller, Pfeifle and other area families.

Ranchers were moving back farther into the mountains beyond the Calaveras Valley and the Arroyo Honda, back into the unfenced, trailless wilderness that stretched all the way to the San Joaquin Valley.

This was country slashed by rocky canyon and crowned by pine-fringed mountain peaks, where rare giant manzanita grew beside ancient oaks, where madrone and

Hotel Site and Livery Stable, Milpitas, Cal.

Livery stable and site of burned hotel (right) on Main Street.

46

laurel-shaded springs fed year-round streams.

This was cattle country and every other section (640 acres) was government land waiting to be homesteaded.

The only name on this remote mountain country on the early maps was Charles McLaughlin, owner of the "railroad lands" spaced between the government sections.

McLaughlin, stagecoach tycoon who later was construction man for the Western Pacific that ran through Milpitas, was paid in land instead of money, In order to finance the railroads, the federal government allowed the states to turn over land to the railroads.

McLaughlin died in 1883...shot by a subcontractor to whom he owed $40,000...but the sections back in the mountains east of Milpitas were retained by the family up into the 20th century.

Before getting into railroading, McLaughlin had helped organize the California Stage Co. which provided service between San Jose and Oakland in the early 1850s, with stops at Milpitas.

Incidentally, the man who shot McLaughlin was exonerated and awarded the $40,000 from McLaughlin's estate.

The early stockmen who took up land in the mountains packed in the lumber for their houses and barns on sleds. They built their own furniture, sometimes out of oak or digger pine growing on their homesteads.

Visits to town were months apart and neighbors were a long horseback ride away; consequently there wasn't a lot of social life for the mountain folk.

Because the pioneer ranchers brought their families, there had to be a school.

Oak Ridge School, hugging the side of the mountain high on the ridge for which it was named east of the Arroyo Honda, opened in 1880 and lasted probably less than a dozen years.

Teachers from 1880 to 1886 were Stephen Hilton and Sarah Smith, and trustees were Jerry Arnold, Mrs. C.W. Swan, E.G. Wilson and William W. Parks.

The roll of honor for Oak Ridge School in August, 1886, as printed in the San Jose *Mercury,* listed Minnie, Josie and Albert Wilson, Nettie and Eva Swall, and Archie, Minnie and Will Parks...probably just about the whole student body.

When ranch youngsters got big enough to work cattle and handle major ranch chores, school was over for most of them.

Few if any went on to high school, which would have meant boarding during the week or the entire term in San Jose or Santa Clara, as there was no high school closer.

Some of the best known of the early back country ranchers were the Parks, Beverson, Ingleson and Valpey families, who stayed longer and left their names on many of the landmarks that still survive.

William Parks came out from New York in 1877 and first settled in Los Gatos, finally moving across the valley and up into Oak Ridge in 1880. His eight young ones (the ninth, Mark, was born on the ridge ranch) may have been the convincer as far as the need for a school was concerned.

Several of the Parks boys continued running cattle in the mountains for many years. "Willie" (William W. Parks) grew up to run cattle on some 14,000 acres of Spring Valley Water Co. land in the same mountains where he went to school. He and his brother, Sam, operated the Milpitas Hotel (later name for French's hostelry) after the turn of the century.

Mark and Arch Parks worked for the vast William Randolph Hearst ranching interests in Mexico and San Simeon. Martha (little Minnie of the 1886 honor roll) grew up to marry Bob Ingleson whose ranch was a few hundred yards above the old Oak Ridge School site.

Charles Beverson, native of Germany, owned more

48

than a thousand acres on the sunrise side of the Arroyo Honda by the late 1880s, and had built a cabin on his land beyond Valpey Creek, remnants of which remain.

Nearby is the stone corral on the property of Capt. Calvin Valpey who died in 1880. The corral, later part of the Lee Ogier holdings, is said to have been built by Indians and may have been there before the Captain homesteaded the land. For years the corral was used at roundup time when ranchers gathered cattle from as far as the San Joaquin.

Others who ran cattle on these lonely mountains included David and Tom Williams, who also had a soda works business in San Jose under the name of Williams Bros.; John Rogge, native of Germany, whose tiny cabin still stands beside Alameda Creek; John Richard Parker from Illinois and the Irishman John Patton.

The other two little rural schools, Calaveras and Laguna, were still holding their own with more than a dozen youngsters in each, with additions during the harvest season.

Teachers at Calaveras School in the 1880s included Nellie Keaton, Lucy Bodley, Ruth M. Thompson and Mrs. S.E. Holyer. Trustees were Dudley Wells and John Carrick.

Teachers at Laguna included Rosalie O'Brien, P. Henning, Miss Emma Watkins, George Kraft, T.W. Whitehurst and Stella Herndon, while trustees were J.W. Greenfield, Alfred Felter, Michael Hughes and H.H. Flagg.

Down in Milpitas proper, the grammar school enjoyed an average attendance of 100, and trustees were J.R. Weller and two men, Samuel Ayer and Edward Topham, whose youngsters together numbered 16.

Entertainment in the 1880s consisted of stage plays, fairs, rodeos, dances, minstrel shows and the like. The Germania Society's masquerade balls in San Jose were popular. The Native Sons of the Golden West, IOOF and other fraternal organizations scheduled railroad

49

Stone corral on Valpey ranch in mountains east of Alameda Creek. Patricia Loomis photo 1970.

excursions, balls and picnics.

Milpitans were among the some 4,000 who attended the Golden Wedding party of Mr. and Mrs. Martin Murphy in 1881 at their home in what later became Sunnyvale.

There was a dance in the new Berryessa School Jan. 25, 1884, and three nights later the New Tivoli Theater (formerly Music Hall) in San Jose opened with a minstrel show.

Among the stage stars that played San Jose's California Theater on S. Second Street in the '80s were Edwin Booth, Louise Davenport, Nat Goodwin, Mrs. John Drew and Frank Bacon.

Milpitans chuckled for several days in January, 1884, over the story of Henry Abel's burglar.

According to a newspaper account, a burglar slipped in the front door of the Abel home on Main Street and made off with a purse containing money and jewelry while the family was having its noon dinner at the rear of the house.

Henry discovered the theft and sounded the alarm. Upon learning a stranger wearing a stovepipe hat had been seen passing through town headed toward San Jose, Henry gave chase.

He apparently caught up with the stovepipe hat and followed at a discreet distance until reaching the streets of San Jose where he found a police officer and had the man arrested.

Upon arriving at the jail, it was learned the Milpitas constable had arrested the man with the purse and had recovered its contents. The newspaper account does not report what Henry Abel said to the stranger in the stovepipe hat, or what the latter said to Henry.

Apparently the San Jose *Mercury* had a Milpitas correspondent in the late 1880s who infrequently sent in items labeled "Milpitas Miscellany."

In one such dated Dec. 28, 1888, the "news" was a new piano "for the hall here," the lease of the hotel stable by Dr. Stark, a veterinary surgeon, who also "talks about constructing a race track in the vicinity," and the death of Henry Topham, former Milpitas hay and grain merchant, in Oakland where he was engaged in the grocery business.

Chapter V

A real estate boom that did not touch Milpitas, and the Spanish-American War that only brushed the little community were major happenings in California during the 1890s.

The town that began in the mid-1850s was still strung out along Main Street, serving the farmers and ranchers minding "the little cornfields" and the big fields of grain, strawberries and vegetables that stretched out in all directions.

Only a few miles away real estate promoters were busy selling off lots in the dream city of New Chicago on the mud flats north of Alviso. A watch factory, stolen from Southern California, was going to be the nucleus of this new city-by-the-bay, but it was not to be, and half a century later New Chicago lots cluttering the tax rolls were still home only to burrowing owls and jackrabbits.

The war came late in the decade, along with the excitement of the Alaskan gold rush, the first automobiles, and a murder case involving a Milpitas lawman.

Earlier in the '90s economic depression spread across the nation, and a railroad strike in 1894 affected shipping of produce. Milpitas residents viewed the aurora borealis in May, 1892, and in June they read in the San Jose Mercury the county's scaffold, no longer needed because the new state law had switched hangings to San Quentin, was being dismantled and sent to Sonoma County for the hanging of a man sentenced before the new law went into effect.

Main Street in Milpitas mid-1890s.

Also in June, 1892, a newspaper item described the play put on by the children of Laguna School. The production, written by the teacher, E.W. Parker, "starred" Will Berry, Lottie Blanch, Ida Harrison, James Fernell, Frank Berry, Nellie, Nettie and Willis Miller, and was a great success, according to the news item.

A description written for the *San Jose Mercury* souvenir book, "Sunshine, Fruit and Flowers," 1896, reaffirms the little town "is one of the most important shipping points in the county."

Mentioned are the strawberries grown by Chinese on land rented for about $20 an acre per year; asparagus averaging about 100 boxes to the acre and yielding a profit of $100 to $300 an acre. "From 12 to 15 carloads of potatoes and green peas are shipped daily from Milpitas during the height of the season," the book says.

By the 1890s dairying was big business for some Milpitans, including Joseph Weller, Charles Beverson and Michael Bellew, along with a newcomer, Joseph F. George, native of the Azores Islands who came to the Milpitas area via Half Moon Bay in 1894.

Some of the business houses in town had different owners, but it was about the same assortment of saloons, general stores and blacksmith shops. New in the 1890s were a drug store operated by Mr. and Mrs. Nicholas Trubschenck, a telephone office and (late in the decade) a cannery.

Saloon keepers included Jose A.P. Cabral and John J. Schemmerhorn; Patrick Condon was supervisor of the Almshouse; Antonio Flores and Jose De Simas had barbershops; Michael F. Haley and the Abels were in the meat business; Jacklin Bros. (J.E. and W.R.) were operating a general store in Milpitas and acting as agents for Wells Fargo Express. Also with general stores were Antonio Cunha and the firm of Topham and Carlo.

Milpitas had a doctor, believed to be the town's first. The name of Dr. William L. Wilson, "Physician and

Laguna School student body in 1898, including five of the Benjamin Gordon family. Clyde Arbuckle photo.

Surgeon" first appears in the 1893 county directory. It last appears in 1904.

Alfred French had retired and was living in San Jose when the decade opened, and C.W. King, who had previously operated a saloon in Mayfield, was proprietor of the hotel until 1895 when Lewis N. Hobbs took over and in 1897 changed the name to Milpitas Hotel.

Alexander Crabb, son of a Portuguese sailor who landed in San Francisco in 1852 and became a San Leandro farmer, came to Milpitas in 1891 as station agent for the then owner of the railroad, the Southern Pacific.

Justices of the peace during the 1890s were E.W. Darling, Henry Batty, Nicholas Trubschenck and A.W. Jones, the latter remaining in this post up into the 20th Century. Constables included Henry B. Lee, F.E. Silva and Frank Pfeifle until 1898 when John Costagan, native of Gilroy and former horse breeder, began his 35-year career as constable,

A man named Matthews, arrested in June, 1898 for murder was reportedly a Milpitas constable, although he is not listed in county records of the period.

Stock farms were thriving in Santa Clara County during the 1890s and up into the new century, these including the famous Elmwood Farm of Charley Boots, reportedly the oldest race horse and breeding farm in California, according to a newspaper article in 1952 when the Boots' 92-year-old colonial mansion on the Alviso-Milpitas Road was torn down.

The farm was developed by Charley's dad, William Boots, but is remembered by oldtimers because of Charley, who was not only known for his race horses, but also for his love and patronage of music, and his hospitality.

The mansion resembled a movie version of "my old Kentucky home." It had two parlors and two music rooms, a circular staircase, massive fireplaces and an eight-foot zinc bathtub.

Among the famous Boots' stallions were Brig O'Doon and Brutus, the latter sire of Lucretia Borgia, a mare that set a record at the old Emeryville track at the turn of the century.

Nutwood was another major horse farm, located near Warm Springs and operated by Martin Carter. George Bollinger, who ran cattle on a thousand acres east of the Arroyo Honda and who served as sheriff early in the decade, was owner of Boodle Roy and the great brood mare speed producer Carrie Benton.

Milpitas in the '90s was touched by happenings of its neighbors and events farther off. There was interest when Leland Stanford, Jr. University opened in 1891, and with the beginnings of Morgan Hill in the subdivision of Hill's 19,000-acre ranch.

There was excitement in 1896 when sheriff's posses prowled the eastern hills looking for James Dunham, wanted for the mass murder of six persons on the McGlincey ranch near Campbell.

Milpitas residents helped San Jose celebrate the 50th anniversary of the meeting of the first state legislature in December, 1899, and they rode the narrow gauge electric cars into Alum Rock Park.

This was the decade that saw the introduction of the Tootsie Roll, Green Stamps and Cracker Jack, founding of the Sierra Club by John Muir, production of the first motor car by a man named Duryea, and publishing of Fannie Farmer's Boston Cooking School cookbook and the first of the Frank Merriwell novels.

The Del Monte label that was to become the leading name in U.S. canned fruits and vegetables was used for the first time in 1891 by the Oakland Preserving Co., which in 1898 built a cannery in Milpitas, principally for processing asparagus, but which also put up tomatoes, beans and other local produce. The first year the output was about 100,000 cases, a report in December, 1899, indicated.

Mail pouch tobacco went on the market in 1897 and its advertising was to decorate barns in Milpitas and elsewhere for more than half a century.

Japanese began arriving in the Santa Clara Valley in the 1890s. They came to work in the seasonal harvests and some stayed to become tenant farmers and eventually to own their own land.

There were some of the same fears and persecutions greeting the arrival of the first Japanese, as in the case of the earlier Chinese, but the feelings were not so intense and there were no major incidents.

Bicycle clubs and race meets were popular in the 1890s, and by mid-decade it was estimated 3,000 bikes were owned by county residents.

By the end of the decade the first horseless carriages were showing up, scaring the buggy horses and scattering chickens on the country roads.

The San Francisco Call May 9, 1896 printed an amusing story of the "historic journey of a horseless carriage through Alameda county...from Oakland to San Jose."

"The vehicle that announces its presence by emitting puffs from the vicinity of the rear wheels has passed through Alameda County, and in those neighborhoods whose commercial life is wrapped up in strawberry beds and potato patches, and where the nearest approach to metropolitan life is a lamp post with coal oil illumination, it has created a great sensation.

"Several minor accidents are also attributed to it and many unnecessary scares have furnished the basis for several stories of narrow escapes from death.

"In Oakland, the machine created genuine surprise, but the citizens suppressed it, not wishing to be taken for residents of the suburbs of Milpitas...

"At Newark, the puffing cart created more sensation than a traveling circus. (Here) Mr. and Mrs. Wills met the snorting phenomenon and their horse at once renounced his allegiance to the reins, broke his harness and injured himself with one of the broken shafts.

"A lady who was driving with her children encountered the carriage and her horse at once bolted.

"At Milpitas the whole population turned out to see the novelty. All through the town the party was tendered an ovation, but there was an agreeable feeling of security when the sound of the puffing had died away. All along the journey there was an indefinable fear that the things might 'go off,' but instead, it went on till it reached San Jose."

The county had nearly 1,000 miles of graded and graveled roads, 350 of which were sprinkled daily in the summer with more than 60 water wagons handling the job. Water was obtained from tanks located along the major county roads at intervals of about 4,000 feet.

Samuel F. Ayer, the county supervisor from Milpitas and an expert on roads, gave a talk at the state convention of county supervisors in Napa in the summer of '98 and advised of the importance of daily sprinkling and quick repair of chuckholes in cutting costs.

"Good roads, well sprinkled, are the best investment any county can make," Ayer said.

The Spanish American War made little impact on Milpitas, or on Santa Clara County as a whole, other than renew patriotic feelings of its citizens and bring about formation of the area's first American Red Cross chapter.

Military companies were formed, eager to go off to fight for the freedom of Cubans and to avenge the destruction of the battleship Maine in the Havana harbor.

There was flag waving and band music as "the Boys" left for the war, which most of them spent at Camp Barrett in San Francisco, and the Red Cross got off to a fine start collecting blankets, underwear, sox and food items for the troops.

Milpitans joined the excitement, although most of the

farmers in the community were probably more concerned with a problem closer to home. The country was in the midst of a drought and artesian wells were drying up, along with streams and springs, bringing economic worries to stockmen and vegetable growers.

Mrs. Samuel Ayer, wife of the county supervisor, was on the original executive committee of the Red Cross in May, 1898, and her son, Henry, was a sergeant in the new Company M of the army volunteers that was formed in Santa Clara County and which also included C.E. Valpey, former storekeeper in Milpitas. Another company, a cavalry regiment known as the California Rangers, was also hastily put together.

Leonard Farrell, who had married Meta Beverson, who grew up on her dad's ranch east of the Arroyo Honda, was a corporal in Co. B when he was mustered into the Eighth Infantry Regiment of California volunteers during the Spanish-American War. He became a colonel in World War I, and later was commissioned a brigadier general by Gov. Earl Warren.

John F. Carey, born and raised in Calaveras Valley until his family moved to San Jose in 1894, joined the California Rangers. He was in the butcher business in East San Jose at the time and in 1903 became a San Jose city councilman.

A.E. Whitton, major in command of Co. M., was from San Jose and was married to the former Mollie Trimble, daughter of the Milpitas pioneer John Trimble.

At least one Milpitas native, Fred Pfeifle, Jr., saw action in the war. In a letter home to his mother, Mrs. Sarah Pfeifle, Fred told of the U.S. forces taking the city of Manila. He was in the Navy and his ship fired on Fort Malata, inflicting much damage and loss of life, and enabling "our soldiers" to storm the fort.

Fred spoke of the beauty of the city, the thickness of the vegetation, the constant rain, and the upcoming liberty "now that we have the city."

Ranches of Miller and Pfeifle (adobe on left) families at bend on Calaveras Road looking west 1880s. Pfeifle family photo.

The Pfeifle family had moved from Laguna Valley into San Jose several years prior to the outbreak of the war.

The summer of 1898 held other excitement for Milpitas residents. Berryessa's only general store burned May 27, and a month later the Milpitas lawman was arrested for murder. He was charged with the fatal shooting of a man who ran when Matthews tried to question him about the theft of the latter's coat and buggy whip.

The case dragged on into November when Matthews was found guilty of manslaughter and sentenced to five years in San Quentin. Aiding in obtaining the lesser sentence was testimony regarding Matthews' good character by such Milpitas citizens as John Carrick, Samuel Ayer, Justice of the Peace A.W. Jones, A.J. Schemmerhorn and James Hansen.

Gold was discovered in Alaska and the rush to the Klondike began in 1897. Thomas W. Healey, a 26-year-old farm boy born in Calaveras Valley, with three companions joined the rush to the gold fields in January, and crammed enough adventure into the next two years to last a lifetime.

The boys ran into their first of several hazardous adventures before their ship got to Seattle. It ran aground and for a time it was feared she would break up and all would be lost. Finally freed, the ship continued safely to port.

The quartet barely made it through Chilcoot Pass when a landslide roared off the mountain, killing 23 men on the trail behind them.

Healey's group had to fell timber to build boats for the long river trip from Lake Bennett to the Yukon and then up the Big Salmon for 150 miles to the gold fields. Healey came down with pneumonia and nearly died as a result of having to sleep on the cold, wet ground.

Healey became a veterinarian, practicing in Santa Clara County for more than 50 years. He was fond of recalling the Klondike adventure but admitted the financial fortunes of the four gold seekers were not in proportion to the physical hardship.

The century closed and Milpitas slid into the 20th Century, still a rural little community not much concerned with its fast-growing big sister to the south...a good place to live and raise a family, where neighbors were friendly and the air clean, where chief concerns were when it would rain, when it would stop raining, who had the fastest horse, and if the old hay press would last another season.

Chapter VI

The first decade of the new century began quietly enough in Milpitas.

A new Southern Pacific Railroad depot was built, R.S. Barber and John Bothelo were pioneering the growing of sugar beets in the area, and shipping them to the sugar refinery at Alvarado.

Veterinarian James Boyd in 1905 built a veterinary hospital on Main Street, and by this time new businesses along the town's central street included Edward P. Giacomazzi's general store, and John F. Smith's saloon at the intersection of the Alviso-Milpitas Road, to be known for 48 years as Smith's Corners.

Milpitas had its second doctor, Renselaer J. Smith, who had come up from Redlands in 1904 to tack up his shingle in Milpitas. He succeeded Dr. William L. Wilson who had served the community 10 years. Dr. Smith was also to become known for his fine collection of butterflies.

A couple of other new names on the Milpitas scene were Frank Dutra who came from Santa Cruz to farm, and E.O. (Sandy) Wool, who acquired a piece of Spring Valley land up on the mountain near the old Mission Peak School.

Pietro (Pete) Covo, native of Italy, bought 160 acres up on Felter Road for $8,000, and planted a vineyard.

About this time Lee Ogier purchased land on the Alameda Creek beyond Black Mountain that had been homesteaded in the 1870s by two brothers, Frederick C. and John A. Green.

John Green died in April, 1900, and, indicative of land and cattle values of the period, his estate was valued at

Feller road, now paved, still passes the John Covo ranch. The original family home at right is still standing.

"about $1,400 for 400 acres of grazing land and about $1,900 for 145 head of cattle."

Tony Flores was joined in his barbershop in 1905 by 19-year-old John (Jack) Gularte, who was later to operate his own shop for 50 years.

Gularte in the 1930s and '40s was a favorite Halloween target of local youths, who traditionally installed an outhouse in front of his barbershop, recalls Bart Sepulveda. Gularte would sit up half the night trying to catch the pranksters, but never did.

In 1908, Joseph Pashote, native of the Azores Islands who had settled at Irvington in the 1880s, came to Milpitas and bought a store and barber shop for his sons, the beginning of the several businesses that were owned and operated by Pashote Brothers for many years. The first stores burned but were rebuilt.

Population of the town was nearly 500 as the century began. Five passenger and two freight trains served Milpitas daily. There was a town hall and two churches, a cannery, William Osterman's grain warehouses, and Henry Abel's meat business which was prosperous enough to warrant running three wagons daily to supply customers around the township.

Fred Lewis Foster, writing for the San Jose *Mercury and Herald* in 1900, described Milpitas and commented on the agriculture of the area.

Foster noted that while other sections of the county had gone ahead of Milpitas in the setting out of orchards, the Milpitas area had surpassed the rest of the county in vegetable growing, and was also known for its hay, grain, cattle and horses.

Vast quantities of milk were shipped out of Milpitas to San Francisco every morning and night, and much beside was hauled to San Jose daily, Foster wrote.

Some of the larger dairy herds were owned by Henry Abel, the O'Toole Produce Co., and Michael Lynn. Among the larger grain and hay ranches were those of George Bollinger, Alexander Rose, Henry Ayer and the Sinnott brothers.

The fact that there were some orchards in the Milpitas area was indicated by Foster who wrote "the Holmes dryer in the Berryessa area shipped about 70 carloads of cured fruit from Milpitas last season."

Jackrabbit Park was a popular picnic spot on the Coyote Creek at the Alviso-Milpitas road crossing. The town held picnics there every other year for the "hill people" up in Laguna and Calaveras valleys, and they in turn held picnics to which the Milpitans were invited.

Heavy frost damaged crops throughout the county late in April, 1901, and Milpitas reported ice. Heavy rains following the cold snap damaged hay crops in the foothills.

Early in the century residents around Milpitas saw their first opossum. The little grey animals with the skinny tails were shipped in from their native Virginia by former residents of that state who were hungry for the taste of roast 'possum. The little critter liked its new home and multiplied rapidly.

Displaced Virginians were not the only folks who relished 'possum, according to the late Gene Vennum who grew up in Berryessa and remembers trapping 'possum along Penitencia and Coyote Creeks for Chinese in San Jose, who gave a dollar apiece for them.

That was, Gene said, "until like most young inexperienced merchants, we became over anxious to make our fortunes and flooded the market, so the price dropped to 20 cents."

With the long walk or bike ride into San Jose and the low price, 'possum trapping lost its appeal for Vennum and his buddies.

The habitual peace and quiet of Milpitas was broken on the morning of April 18, 1906, by the roar and rumble and shaking of the big earthquake that was to be used as a yardstick for all the earthquakes to come in the next half century.

Milpitas suffered damage, but nothing like the wreckage at nearby Agnews Insane Asylum, and at San Francisco, San Jose and Palo Alto.

Nearly every chimney in Milpitas was knocked down by the jolt and many water tanks were toppled. Milpitas had no skyscrapers and its buildings were wood or adobe, and thus suffered only minor damage.

The Milpitas Hotel slipped on its foundation, and supports on the Alviso-Milpitas bridge over the Coyote Creek were damaged, rendering the bridge unsafe for travel.

Cracks six inches wide showed up in various places, including the Boots ranch west of town. Mrs. North Whitcomb's place on the south side of the Alviso-Milpitas road east of Coyote Creek had cracks a foot wide. Also noticed at this latter place were prune trees in the orchard two to six feet out of alignment.

Immediately after the earthquake water was seen to gush from some of the cracks on the Boots' ranch and elsewhere, shooting up half a foot or more and piling up sand to a height of six inches.

People living near the Coyote said the water in the creek rose between two and three feet immediately after the earthquake, and it was more than a week before the water returned to normal levels.

A quarter of a mile north of the Alviso-Milpitas Road bridge the road along the west side of the Coyote was shoved east into the channel of the creek, and with it a number of willow and cottonwood trees. One of the largest cracks in this area was five feet wide, six feet deep and over 100 feet long.

At the few residences remaining in Calaveras Valley, the chimneys toppled. Robert Ingleson whose ranch was on the ridge east of the little valley reported springs near his

John Sinnott home in the late 1800s. Sinnott family photo.

house increased their flow about four times the usual amount and remained muddy for two or three days.

Several people died in San Jose, including a member of the O'Toole family staying at the Vendome Hotel on N. First Street, and at Agnews Insane Asylum 112 persons lost their lives in the collapse of the brick hospital.

Years later Mrs. Charles Beverson had no trouble remembering the earthquake. She said the chimney in the two-story house on the Oakland road south of Milpitas fell, but the worst damage was in the pantry and the tank house.

The pantry was floating in milk left standing in nine pans the night before, while out in the tank house bottles of catsup made the previous day broke and mixed with water from the broken water tank.

In the red mess drowned and half-drowned baby chicks floated. "They (her husband and daughter, Meta) saddled their horses and raced off to town, leaving me with all the mess," Mrs. Beverson remembered in an interview on her 100th birthday in 1954.

Aloyse Sinnott, Ethel Murphy and Maude Arnold, granddaughters of John Sinnott, recalled the excitement of the 1906 earthquake in an interview in 1976.

"A man named Casey was the dairyman on the Sinnott ranch and he was milking when the 'quake came. He found himself out in the field with a bucket of milk in his hand among all the cows. They had just broken their stanchions and panicked. He put the bucket down and we heard him calling "Mae, Ethel, Maude, are you all right?'

"We couldn't talk, we were so terrified. He tried to get into the house to save us. The house had just moved off its foundation a bit, and the chimney was gone.

"In the parlor there were portraits, not small ones, of the relatives, and their faces were all turned to the wall. The water tank fell down and missed the house by six feet. It roared when it went because the tank was lined with tin. It didn't do any harm, just wiped the yard clean."

71

With the stepped-up purchase of watershed lands by Spring Valley Water Co. prior to beginning construction of Calaveras Dam, farmers were moving out and the enrollment of the 1862 Calaveras School dropped drastically, forcing its abandonment.

The district merged with Laguna School District on June 20, 1904. Among the last teachers at Calaveras were Claire E. Boyce and Amy Wigmore, daughters of Milpitas blacksmiths.

Already increased population in little Laguna Valley and its surrounding hills had brought the need for another school. Airpoint District was formed March 17, 1903 out of portions of Laguna and Milpitas districts. Petitioners for the school included James Hansen. He had attended Laguna School as a youngster and was now farming in the area. His wife was Euphenia, daughter of neighbor Frederick Brandt. The latter's son, Charles Brandt, was a member of Laguna School board for 13 years.

The new school was located at the northeast corner of the intersection of Downing and Calaveras Roads, and the first teacher was Mary Moellering. George Lucas Downing was a long-time trustee of Airpoint School.

New communitites were coming into being: Sunnyvale, Los Altos and Monte Vista. Libbey, McNeill & Libby built the Sunnyvale plant which would become the world's largest canning and freezing facility.

A.P. Giannini, Alviso native, founded the Bank of Italy in San Francisco in 1904. In 1908 the Model T. Ford was introduced, General Motors Co. was founded, and Muir Woods National Monument was established.

Osen and Hunt in San Jose turned out their first automobiles and Frank Holmes was manufacturing the Sunset automobile and touring around in the 1898 Stanley Steamer that was the first car into Yosemite, driven by Frank and his brother.

Professor John J. Montgomery was experimenting with heavier-than-air gliders, but was beaten out by the

Wright brothers in achieving gasoline-powered flight.

Milpitans went in to San Jose in 1901 to welcome President McKinley, who upon his assassination a few months later was honored with a statue in St. James Square financed by money San Jose had collected for an art gallery.

Vaudeville had "found" Milpitas and comedians on the Orpheum Circuit couldn't resist jokes about the little town.

Taken in by the jokes was Amaury Mars, a Frenchman who visited Milpitas in 1901 after hearing "wondrous tales...of a museum, a cathedral, of ancient ruins..."only to find "some houses, a railroad station, drug store, blacksmith shop and the inevitable saloons."

The early years of the new century saw the beginning of one little cemetery and the abandonment of another.

St. John the Baptist Cemetery beside Piedmont Road is part of 6.50 acres of land sold by Frederico and Teresa Narvaez to Sebina G. Dias Sept. 8, 1898 for $625 "in gold coin." Four days later, on September 12, she sold the property to the Roman Catholic Archbishop of San Francisco for the same price, according to title company records.

The little sun-baked cemetery, its headstones rising out of the brick-hard adobe amid a few shrubs and trees, shrank to less than three acres because of sale of a piece to a neighbor in 1927 and deeding of footage for realignment of Piedmont Road in 1938.

The graveyard was laid out in September, 1900, as a parish cemetery for St. John the Baptist Church in Milpitas, and was blessed on Sept. 7, 1902.

The first burial according to cemetery records was that of John Joseph Cabral, 55, native of Portugal, and occurred Feb. 13, 1903.

There are over 100 burials in the little cemetery, although not that many headstones.

Names on the headstones recall the early Portuguese

immigrants who found new roots in the foothills and fertile farmland surrounding Milpitas, and who helped make the area famous for its early spring peas, potatoes, and other vegetables.

These names include Borge, Carlo, Coehlo, Gomes, Lopes, Mello, Nunes, Pashote, Pedro, Rose, Silva, Silveira, Soares and Terra, without whom the history of Milpitas could not be written.

The other little cemetery was on a hillside in Laguna Valley, a little two-acre plot shaded by oaks and laurels and a row of poplars planted many years ago.

The first burials were in the early 1860s and on Feb. 25, 1871, the Laguna Cemetery was deeded by Albert D. Smith to David Campbell, Thomas Sox and Josiah Evans as trustees. The last burial was in 1914 and for many years afterwards Weller Curtner paid the taxes on the little graveyard to preserve the last resting places of friends and neighbors of his grandparents.

A faded map of the cemetery, laid out in alleys and avenues running between the grave plots, indicates most of the plots had been sold by 1867, although some had already changed hands. An Ayer plot had been sold to Healey and P. Mathews had sold part of a plot to J.M. Gregory.

Other names on the map included Josiah Evans, William Carson, J.H. Miller, C. Valpey, David Campbell, J.H. Dooley, J. Weller, William Reed, J. Carrick, Felter and Pomeroy.

By the 1950s only a few headstones remained, and in the early 1970s the cemetery would become part of Ed Levin County Park.

The headstones, now nearly all gone, told the sad story of death in childbirth, infants who succumbed to illnesses, and of men and women not yet old in years.

The epitaph for Beneville Kime Reed, 31, who died of a heart attack April 17, 1867 while riding horseback with two companions, read:

"Young people all, as you pass by,
As you are now, so once was I.
As I am now, so you will be.
Prepare for death and follow me."

Early in August, 1910, fire destroyed the Milpitas Hotel, three saloons, two barbershops and a grocery store, according to an item in the San Jose *Mercury Herald*. Damages were estimated at $25,000, and heaviest losers were W.W. Parks, Pashote Bros., Tony Flores and Frank Terra.

A bucket brigade was formed under leadership of Constable John Costigan which managed to save the livery stable behind the hotel.

The newspaper noted Milpitas has absolutely no fire protection, mentioning the recent destruction of the cannery by fire at a loss of about $100,000.

Milpitas and Airpoint schools both entered floats in the 1910 Carnival of Roses in San Jose. The Milpitas float was pulled by six grey horses and was accompanied by the Milpitas Band.

Workmen are clearing the Calaveras Valley floor to prepare for the construction of a dam. (San Francisco Water Co. photo)

Chapter VII

World War occupied almost everybody in one way or another in the second decade of the 20th Century. Milpitans joined the fighting forces sent overseas and those who stayed home helped in the war bond drives and the Red Cross campaigns.

School children planted vegetable gardens and women rolled bandages and knitted sweaters and sox for the "boys in the trenches."

Nellie Evans was a lieutenant-colonel heading up the Milpitas sector of the Women's Mobilized Army, a fund-raising group, and others served on draft boards, in the Council of Defense, and other committees.

Mrs. Edith Daley, San Jose librarian who wrote the war history of Santa Clara County lists many from Milpitas who had an active part.

These include G.L. Downing, Miss Nellie Evans, Henry M. Ayer, G.E. Abel, Lawrena Baker, A.L. Crabb, Lawrence Hansen, Mr. and Mrs. E.P. Giacomazzi, Dr. R.J. Smith, A.M. Silva, Jr., Miss Gertrude Abel, Miss Elizabeth Weller, Miss M. Topham, Mrs. Elsie Abel, Mrs. Charles Beverson and daughter, Meta, Edith Ayer, Miss Annie Rose and Miss Mae Curtner.

Irving Crabb, son of the banker and early S.P. ticket agent, was one of Milpitas' native sons serving in the Army.

Others who served and died, and whose names later were affixed to a war memorial marker on Main Street, included Johnny Edward Pashote, brothers Manuel R. and Joseph I. Rose.

In 1930, Mrs. Louise Rose, only Gold Star mother in Maj. Randolph T. Zane Auxiliary, Veterans of Foreign Wars, was invited to place a wreath on the grave of France's unknown soldier because she had lost two sons.

World War began in Europe in 1914. The United States declared war on Germany April 6, 1917 and Gen. John J. Pershing was recalled from Mexico where he was commanding an American force chasing Pancho Villa.

During the decade of the 'teens, the S.S. Titanic sank after hitting an iceberg in the North Atlantic, the 16th amendment to the Constitution empowered Congress to levy taxes on incomes above $3,000 a year.

Hetch Hetchy dam on the Tuolumne River was funded in 1913 to provide water and hydroelectric power for San Francisco; parcel post service was inaugurated; the Panama Canal opened to traffic; the Workmen's Compensation Act was passed; Congress created the National Park Service; President Woodrow Wilson in 1916 won a second term on the slogan "He kept us out of war."

The decade drew to a close amidst much labor unrest, strikes and race riots; passage of the 19th amendment in 1919 giving women the right to vote; outbreak of Spanish influenza which took many lives in Santa Clara County and across the nation.

It was a decade when war songs such as "Over There," "Keep the Home Fires Burning" and "You're in the Army Now" were popular, and Hollywood was turning out films starring Douglas Fairbanks, Dorothy Gish, Wallace Beery and Charlie Chaplin, as well as the Keystone Cops with Roscoe "Fatty" Arbuckle.

The second wave of Mexican Americans began arriving in the Milpitas area, and among the first was Juan Cervantez (uncle of Josephine (Camarillo) Guerrero), about 1914.

In July, 1913, nearly 40 years after Spring Valley Water

Co. purchased the first farm in Calaveras Valley in the mid-1870s, construction began on the dam at the north end of the little valley that would create a reservoir holding 32 billion gallons of water for residents of San Francisco.

The farms that covered the valley floor and ranged up into the surrounding hills had been purchased one by one since 1876. Lawsuits brought an end to the buying, but not before Spring Valley Water Co. had acquired 40,000 acres of watershed in Southern Alameda County and northern Santa Clara County.

The late Frazier O. Reed, through the Clayton real estate office, bought most of the parcels purchased between 1908 and 1913, from as far north as Dublin and Livermore and as far south as Mt. Hamilton. The properties were purchased in many different names in an effort to keep land owners from realizing the San Francisco water company was gobbling up the countryside.

Reed recalled long days covering the rugged mountain country in a horse and buggy, carrying his saddle in the buggy so he could switch to horseback when the wagon tracks petered out or when the creeks were running high.

The late Weller Curtner remembered Fred Herrmann of the famous San Jose surveying family (Herrmann Bros., surveyors and civil engineers, made the first complete map of Santa Clara County in the 1870s) did the survey work for the dam. Water company records indicate Herrmann was hired as construction engineer in 1910 and a year later was appointed chief engineer for Spring Valley, working on the firm's other projects as well as Calaveras.

Old timers remember rails were laid up Calaveras Road and across the deserted farms on the floor of Calaveras Valley in order to bring up the steam shovel needed to build the dam.

"I remember the fuss at the Milpitas depot when they rolled the steam shovel off the train," Curtner said. Frank

A January, 1924 view of the Calaveras Dam construction. A train track was laid to help provide the 2.3 million cubic yards of material. (San Francisco Water Co. photo)

80

Pedro was a youngster attending Airpoint School and remembers with awe watching the train inch its way up the road past the school.

"They used monitors to wash in the fine stuff and let it settle after they put up the sides of the dam," Curtner recalled. "Mules were used to haul dump buckets."

When the dam was nearing completion early in 1918, it was said to be the largest earthfill dam in the world and had cost $2,500,000.

On March 24, 1918, 600,000 cubic feet of earth slid from the dam into the reservoir destroying a 235-foot concrete tower housing the flood gate machinery and causing an estimated $500,000 in damage.

The slide moved to the south, into the reservoir and 60 feet of water, blocking the tunnel outlet and preventing a rush of water down on Sunol and the country to the north.

Thirty-eight wagons and a section of the railroad used in the construction work went down with the slide.

Work was immediately begun to repair the damage, but it took until 1925 to complete.

Only six months after the disaster to Calaveras dam, another catastrophe struck. This time it was rain, more than six inches of it, which poured down on Santa Clara Valley September 12 and 13, 1918, just as the prune harvest was at its peak.

Prunes lay like a purple carpet in orchards all over the valley, only a small percentage of the crop having been picked and set out on trays to dry.

The torrential rain turned the tilled earth in the orchards into deep mud and the prunes lay on the ground molding and fermenting until as San Jose City Historian Clyde Arbuckle described it, "the whole valley smelled like a distillery in distress."

Soldiers from Camp Fremont up the Peninsula were brought down, and volunteers rallied to try to save the crop. The government had arranged to purchase

81

First bank in Milpitas early 1920s. Florence Lee (Ogier) Hawley photo.

approximately 20,000,000 pounds of Santa Clara Valley prunes, the largest single order ever placed for the fruit in this area, and most of it was to be sent overseas for the military.

The war work council and San Jose Chamber of Commerce helped recruit labor, but the men could not get into the orchards, and the prunes, and many acres of ripening tomatoes rotted.

The disaster resulted in the construction of dehydrators, so the whims of Mother Nature would not again cost orchardists so dearly.

Some of the better things that happened during this second decade of the 1900s included the paving of the Oakland (Milpitas) Road from San Jose to the Alameda County line, beginning in 1914. Electricity finally arrived in Milpitas in 1911, brought in by PG&E, and the Milpitas Improvement Club was formed in 1912 with Dr. James Boyd as president.

The Bank of Milpitas was established in 1911, Alexander Crabb and Edward P. Giacomazzi having a hand in the effort.

Floods inundated much of the valley in early March, 1911, and George Files, who operated a tavern on the Alviso Road west of Milpitas was forced to evacuate when the overflow from the Guadalupe River and Coyote Creek began spilling over his polished bar. A launch worked its way overland and rescued him, but the current was so strong the craft was unable to buck the flow and Files spent the night in Alviso.

Up stream on the Coyote 150 head of hogs and a few cows were swept from their pens at the Wendt slaughterhouse near Berryessa and carried through the Milpitas area.

The late Joe Simas could remember a walk down Main Street in 1914. Beginning at Weller Lane and walking south, the First Presbyterian Church stood on what later was the old city hall parking lot. There was a blacksmith shop, then Topham's machine shop where Madruga Iron Works stood in after years.

Dr. Boyd's veterinary hospital was on the location of the later Cracolice department store, and Pashote Bros. occupied the site of the Kozy Kitchen restaurant.

The Milpitas Hotel was on the northwest corner of Main and the Alviso-Milpitas Road, site of the future Fat Boy Barbeque, and Smith's corners across the street was to become Campbell's Corners, Simas recalled.

The cannery occupied the site of the later Milpitas Liquors and professional center, with the Bank of Milpitas (later Bank of America) across the street. William Osterman's warehouse was just down Main, and the post office of the 1940s was between Gularte's barbershop and the Milpitas Drug Store, remembers Bart Sepulveda.

Frank Krusich was selling Fords and operating a garage in Milpitas, keeping up with the transition from hayburner to gasburner. Elmer M. Whelpley had the Milpitas Lumber Co. and Frank Bothelo and Fred W. Nohl were defying the inevitable and had opened blacksmith shops in town.

Milpitas farmer Edward Sakauye bought one of Krusich's Fords and still owned it decades later. Extra accessories and so forth brought the price to roughly $620, he remembers.

In April, 1912, the Milpitas School burned and a temporary building was erected on Railroad Avenue, which was used until a new school was completed in June, 1916.

A small school building saved from the flames in 1912 was sold to Frank Krusich for $365 and served as a garage for many years.

Principal when the new school held its first classes was Anthony Texeria.

Joe Lial is listed in the 1918 Santa Clara County

directory as operating the Farmers' Saloon in Milpitas where he gave out tokens good for one free drink.

During this decade steelhead weighing up to 20 pounds could still be speared in Penitencia Creek, according to the late Gene Vennum who remembered the pitchfork forays in the Berryessa area. He also recalled the entire east side of the valley from Alviso and Milpitas to Evergreen was overrun with pheasants.

Judge S.F.Leib who had a ranch on Lundy Road in Berryessa imported the birds early in the century and when the flock got too large he turned them loose to multiply in the overgrown ditches and along the Penitencia and Coyote creeks. Vennum said although it was against the law to shoot the birds, many found their way to the tables of local farmers. Changing agricultural methods contributed mainly to their demise, but there were still some of the birds decades later.

Many of the old pioneer names were still on the land they or their parents settled a half-century before.

County directories at the outset of the 1920s still listed such names as Abel, Ayer, Barber, Bellew, Carrick, Downing, Sepulveda, Chavarria, Murphy, Parks, Rose, Spangler, Weller, Shearer, Simas, Russell, Evans and Sherman.

Frank H. Topham was justice of the peace and John Costigan was constable as the decade began, and when it ended Joseph M. Bellew was the justice and Costigan was still the law in Milpitas. Both served until Milpitas township was annexed to San Jose in 1922.

July 4 parade early 1920s. Florence Lee (Ogier) Hawley photo.

86

Chapter VIII

The decade of the 1920s is remembered as the period in which America survived bathtub gin and the stock market crash, Aimee Semple McPherson and the Charleston.

It was a period marked by momentous world events unrecognized at the time, but remembered a few years later...the coming to power of Benito Mussolini, Adolph Hitler and Josef Stalin, men whose fanatical beliefs would affect a generation of world citizens.

The 1920s were exciting for the advancement in the electronic medium, automobile production, Charles Lindbergh's and Amelia Earhart's solo flights across the Atlantic, the beginning of U.S. airmail service, and the discovery of King Tut's tomb.

Babe Ruth hit home run number 60, establishing a record that would hold for 30 years. Lawrence Welk put together a dance band, Gallant Fox won the Triple Crown of horse racing, and a Palo Alto man named Herbert Hoover was elected president of the United States.

A new comic strip, "Little Orphan Annie," showed up; the Maidenform brassiere was introduced, sparking passing comments down at the Spangler and Crabb garage or in Pashote's grocery store. Frank Krusich was promoting sale of Ford's new touring car at the affordable price of $290.

In 1927 Santa Clara Valley growers, the D'Arrigo brothers, were the first in the United States to grow broccoli.

Load of hay on E.O. Wool ranch early 1920s. Wool family photo.

And Milpitas was getting new businesses. Beside Krusich's Ford dealership, the Fat Boy Barbecue arrived midway through the decade, John A. Carlo opened a dry goods store, Joe Stemel was running the Harry Morris Co. grain business, and in 1928 a young man named Sal Cracolice came to operate the drug store.

The Winsor family built a new blacksmith shop on Main Street, Clyde House opened an auto repair shop and Henry L. Sutherland had a harness business.

The Western Pacific Railroad (no relative of the 1859 road which became the Southern Pacific) ran its line through Milpitas from Niles to San Jose early in the decade, giving the town two railroads.

The Western Pacific bought five acres of Charles Brandt's 12-acre parcel on Calaveras Road in Milpitas in 1920, building its depot and laying out station yards early in 1922. (Brandt, born on the family ranch in Calaveras Valley in the 1860s, owned several ranches, including a prune orchard on Capitol Avenue south of Milpitas.)

Other orchardists during this period included Joe Cuciz who had apricots on Piedmont Road on land that included the old Alviso adobe, across from which John Sepulveda, descendant of Jose Maria Alviso, grew prunes and apricots; Allan and Miles Standish's pear orchard on the Coyote Creek north of the Alviso-Milpitas road; E.O. (Sandy) Wool, John Chavarria (his dad had planted one of the first walnut orchards in the area), William M. Curtner, Alfred Gallagher, George Nicholson and William Bellew.

Some of the smaller justice courts had been losing money for years (only Morgan Hill was operating in the black) and on June 8, 1922, the county board of supervisors voted to consolidate some of these townships, effective Jan. 1, 1923.

Milpitas, which spent $2,000 and only took in $17 in the past year, and Alviso townships were absorbed by San

Well drilling on Ayer ranch around 1918. Florence Lee (Ogier) Hawley photo.

Jose. The action marked the end of the long careers of Milpitas Judge Joe Bellew and Constable John Costigan.

Also in the decade aerial circuses were popular and one that old timers long remembered was the Feb. 22, 1922 show staged from a field at White and Tully Toads in which famed air acrobat Thornton A. (Jinx) Jenkins was killed when his parachute failed to open.

Other entertainment during the 20s included big July 4 celebrations, complete with parade and barbeque, the Holy Ghost fiestas, Saturday night dances in Maple Hall above Pashote's grocery (later the drug store) and (from 1926 on) the Fiesta de las Rosas held in San Jose each May.

In the 1927 Fiesta, Milpitas rancher Lucas Downing was aide to Grand Marshal Louis Oneal in the parade, and County Supervisor Henry M. Ayer rode in one of the decorated automobiles.

In the historic museum display Charles Boots exhibited pictures of his home place, Elmwood, and of his famed racing mare, Lucretia Borgia. He also loaned for exhibit a driving whip and Victoria that had come "around the Horn," along with his father's journal of 1852.

Mrs. R.A. Costigan (nee House) displayed a Spanish shawl in the family since 1847, Mrs. E.C. Reed (formerly Margaret Trimble) had several items on display in the museum, including brass candlesticks, a handwoven bed spread, and a daguerrotype taken of some of the family before leaving Missouri to come overland to California in 1849.

Wagons and buggies competed with automobiles on Main Street in Milpitas and there was still a water trough in front of Smith's Corners.

Cattlemen still drove their stock down out of the hills to the corrals at the depot, vegetable and grain fields stretched out across the flat lands and up into the hills. Sugar beets had been added to the list of products produced in the area, along with spinach. There were a squab farm and some of the largest dairies in the state.

91

E.O. Wool tomato field on floor of Calaveras Valley late 1920s before dam completed. Wool family photo.

Among the Milpitas dairymen were George Abel, Frank Marty, Manuel Moniz and John Silveria.

In town, Standard Oil Co. built a plant, and in 1929 Pacific Gas & Electric Co. constructed its gas control center, giving the Bay Area its first major source of natural gas.

Calavaras Dam was completed without fanfare in 1925.

Runoff water from creeks tumbling down the wooded canyon in the shadow of Mt. Hamilton and Black Mountain began backing up behind the 775-foot high earthen barricade.

The spreading lake covered the foundations of homes of the early settlers and climbed up the stumps of fruit and shade trees that marked the farms of families named Sherman, Buick, Wells, Campbell and Pomeroy.

Most of the barns and houses and other buildings had been torn down and the lumber hauled away by neighbors, and the trees had been cut down for firewood before the lake began filling up.

Should the lake be drained in later years the stumps, a few fences and foundations would be visible in the silt to remind historians of the early settlement.

The lake wiped out the road which ran the length of the little valley and necessitated construction of the higher road that dodges in and out of the little canyons along the west sides of Calaveras Lake.

The rising water put an end to tomato production which Sandy Wool had been carrying on for several years on the floor of the valley.

The lake rose to cover 1,435 acres and back up nearly 32 billion gallons of water for thirsty San Franciscans. In 1930 Calaveras and the other water sources of Spring Valley Water Co. were sold to the City of San Francisco.

Also during the 1920s another major source of water for San Francisco, and eventually users in the northern section of Santa Clara County, was being developed. O'Shaughnessy dam high up on the icy waters of the

93

Tuolumne River next door to Yosemite was completed in 1923 as a major unit of the Hetch Hetchy system bringing Sierra water across the San Joaquin Valley and into the Bay Area.

There were still deer, coyotes and lions in the mountains, roads were unpaved, and inside plumbing and telephones were "new-fangled" conveniences not everyone had acquired.

Josephine Guerrero remembers the "party lines" which allowed the others on the line to listen in on conversations, picking up "a lot of news that they weren't supposed to get." Mrs. Guerrero recalls most homes in town had electricity, but wood stoves were still the main feature of Milpitas kitchens in the 1920s.

There was still much hay grown in the area, and come June each year would find James P. Dempsey's hay press crew working in the fields with horse-drawn equipment. The six to eight-man crew was paid $4 to $6 for a 16-hour day and traveled from ranch to ranch. They got five meals a day and slept in the hay at night, remembered the late Municipal Judge John F. Dempsey, who worked for his dad summers while he was going to high school and college.

He also remembers the bales weren't the little lightweight kind modern balers turn out, but the ones the old hay crews had to wrestle with weighed 300 pounds or more.

California Packing Corp.'s cannery brought a jump in the population each January and February during the pea harvest, crowding the schools and increasing business for the merchants.

Some Milpitans worked in Tom Foo Chew's Bayside Cannery in Alviso during the summer. Among these was Josephine Simas Carlo who recalls cannery trucks would pick up the workers before sunrise and bring them home at night. She remembers there was a dance every week at the

Milpitas baseball team early 1920s. Elaine Rodgers photo.

cannery and a big party at the end of the season.

Milpitans were on hand for the inauguration of air mail shuttle service between San Jose and Oakland, linking transcontinental service Oct. 15, 1928.

John Johnston flew to Oakland from the airfield at Alum Rock and Capitol Avenue, meeting the eastern planes and returning with the first packets of airmail.

Johnston's plane was berthed at the San Jose field and local officials were required to meet government regulations for the service. These, according to the San Jose *Mercury Herald*, included installation of 20 white lanterns on iron stanchions along the north edge of the field, a red light and spot light on the hanger, and filling in the gopher and squirrel holes in the landing strip.

Another event of 1928 was the campaign to buy 1,000 acres of hayland at Sunnyvale to turn over to the Navy for a dirigible base. Arthur Curtner of Warm Springs, son of pioneer Henry Curtner, was instrumental in the project which raised $470,000 and gave Santa Clara County Moffett Field.

The stock market crash late in 1929 had little effect on the farming community where the major investments were in seed for crops paid for at harvest time when the farmers also settled up their grocery bills and made payments on plows and other equipment.

Chapter IX

In the 1930s refugees from the dust bowl of the midwest poured into Milpitas in battered cars with mattresses on top. They came to pick peas, dig potatoes, work in the orchards and at whatever other farm jobs they could find.

They camped on the hillside farms where they worked, or in the orchards, and on Saturday night they came to town to buy hamburger, shoes, tobacco, beans and oatmeal.

They worked for 15 cents an hour and the weekly paycheck was shy of $10, but it went a long way...far enough to feed and clothe the family and buy gas to move on to the cotton fields and vineyards of the San Joaquin, or the orange groves of Southern California.

These were the depression years, and what was happening in Milpitas was happening all over Santa Clara County, California and the nation.

Dust storms beginning in May, 1934, blew some 300 million tons of Kansas, Texas, Oklahoma and Colorado top soil into the Atlantic and this was only the beginning. Farmers planted and replanted, but the wind blew away the seed. Thousands gave up and headed west, camping along the old overland trail where covered wagons rolled less than a century before, patching tires, and making baling wire repairs to keep moving.

The parents and older children got jobs on the farms wherever they could and the younger children crowded the schools, forcing the hiring of another teacher or two during the harvest season.

The Depression did not hit Milpitas with the impact felt by the large cities. Because it was a farm community its people had food..."People lived, they didn't starve...they got by," recalls Sal Cracolice, who was the druggist in Milpitas during those early Depression years.

"We didn't notice it as much as they did in the cities," Josephine Carlo, Kozy Kitchen's restaurant owner said. "We had cattle, pigs, chickens. My mother had a garden and did a lot of canning. We gave the surplus away. At butchering time all the neighbors helped. Everybody shared."

Dr. Al Currlin came to Milpitas during the Depression in 1935, and he remembers "thousands of itinerant laborers that would move through and set up camp actually on orchards and hillsides.

"There were a lot of babies I delivered in tents...on the sides of the hills with the mother on a mattress and me on my knees."

"If wages were low, so was the price of food and other necessities," Cracolice points out. He remembers buying gasoline for as low as 7 cents a gallon, and bread and milk for pennies.

The national average earnings in 1933 for a doctor were $3,382, $4,218 for a lawyer, $907 for a construction worker, $1,227 for a public school teacher and $216 for a farmhand. Typical food prices were 28 cents a pound for butter, 10 cents a quart for milk, 29 cents a dozen for eggs, 5 cents a loaf for bread, and the pound price was 29 cents for sirloin steak, 2 cents for potatoes, 22 cents for chicken and 29 cents for coffee.

Franklin D. Roosevelt was president and his New Deal saw dozens of organizations created to effect a return to prosperity, such as the Works Progress Administration and the Civilian Conservation Corps. Farmers were paid for not growing crops. The Social Security system went into effect in 1935. There were sit-down strikes and the three-

John Sepulveda and mother (Salena) with ways of drying apricots on Piedmont Road west of St. John the Baptist Cemetery 1934. Bart Sepulveda photo.

month maritime workers' strike which tied up West Coast shipping in 1936.

The "great experiment" known as Prohibition ended late in 1933 with ratification of the 21st Amendment. In the preceding 13 years an estimated 1.4 billion gallons of hard liquor was sold illegally across the nation.

With the end of prohibition, beer-makers and distillers went back into production on a grand scale, and soft drink and ice cream sales dropped dramatically.

The Spanish civil war and the China-Japanese conflict occupied most of the '30s, while the Nazi party grew strong in Germany. U.S. track star Jesse Owens embarrassed Adolph Hitler at the Berlin Olympic games in 1936, beating the Nazi leaders' "pure Aryan" athletes and winning four gold medals.

Boulder (Hoover) Dam was completed on the Colorado River in 1936, the German dirigible Hindenburg exploded and burned May 6, 1937 at Lakehurst, N.J., and two Joes, Louis and Di Maggio, were making news in boxing and baseball.

Sunsweet introduced the first commercial prune juice in 1933, the Golden Gate Bridge opened May 27, 1937, Superman was introduced in comic books in 1938. The following year Permanente Cement Co. was founded by Henry Kaiser to supply material for construction of Shasta Dam, and Hewlett-Packard, Inc. began in Palo Alto.

Closer to home in San Jose were such happenings as the burning of the courthouse May 18, 1931, and the lynching of the kidnappers of Brooke Hart, son of a San Jose department store owner, Nov. 19, 1933.

The business community of Milpitas was busy during the harvest season, but the town did not change much and the population stayed between 300 and 400, while the area it served grew from 1,000 to 2,000 during the months the migratory workers camped on the farms and orchards.

"It was like Saturday all the time" during the harvest season, says druggist Cracolice. "We waited for them (the

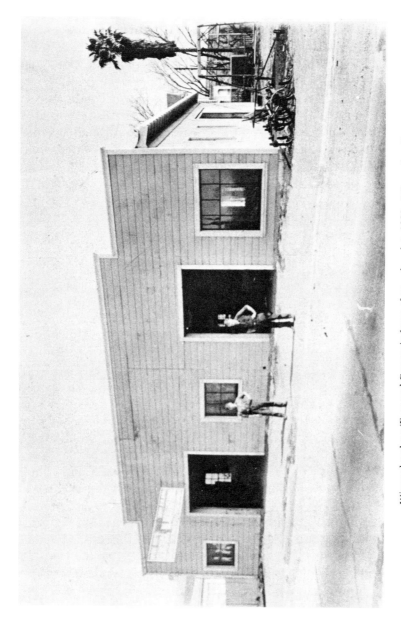

Winsor brothers Tom and George in front of new shop late 1920s. Winsor family photo.

farm workers), we catered to that portion of business that time of year. I had herbs and things that are unheard of now in drug stores that Mexican people used."

Other things Cracolice remembers about the 1930s was the lack of a water or sewer system, and the many telephone poles..."We called it Poleville more than we did Milpitas."

Tom Cardoza had a grocery store across from the Catholic Church, Frank Amaral had another behind Spangler's Shell Service station east of Main Street that later was run by Pop Mills. Coast Counties Oil Co. and Standard Oil were both in Milpitas in the 1930s, Irving Crabb had the lumber company, Dr. Tom Healey was the veterinarian, Pashote Bros. had a meat market, Rollin J. Rose and F.J. Terra had the T & R Garage, and "the village blacksmith" was still named Winsor.

Milpitas lost one of its historic buildings in April, 1935 when the little 1865 school was torn down. It had been sold to Ford dealer Frank Krusich when the new school was built in 1916 and used as a garage.

There was a baseball field down next to the Almshouse and Milpitas teams played San Jose, Santa Clara and other area teams.

Joseph Smith came to Milpitas in 1930 and remembers the cannery occupied most of the east side of Main Street in town. Jack Pashote's slaughter house was west of Main in the area of the later Calaveras Boulevard and Abel Street.

Smith, who was later to be fire chief of Milpitas City, grew peas, corn and potatoes in the hills east of Piedmont Road, selling most of his harvest right in the field. Vegetables were being grown where the later Ford plant would be located, and just east of the Western Pacific tracks there was a big dairy.

Smith and Cracolice (and others) remember the monstrous traffic jams in Milpitas on weekends. The main routes to Oakland from San Jose and the north and west sides of Santa Clara Valley were the San Jose-Oakland and Alviso-Milpitas roads. Cars would be backed up miles in

102

both directions...sometimes as far south as Murphy's barn and Wayne Station over a mile beyond the Almshouse.

Most popular Saturday night entertainment in the '30s was to drive into San Jose to a movie, maybe a musical with Ginger Rogers and Fred Astaire, or a Shirley Temple film.

The country was climbing out of the Depression as the decade ended, but World War II was about to begin. Hitler marched into Austria and on September 1 while Milpitas hunters were banging away on the first day of the 1939 dove season, Poland was attacked.

Chapter X

Rumblings of war were only faintly heard in Milpitas and across America as the decade of the 1940s began, but they grew louder as Germany invaded Yugoslavia, Greece and Russia in the early half of 1941.

U.S. ships were fired upon by German U-boats in October, and on December 7, 1941, Pearl Harbor was attacked by Japanese planes.

The United States joined the worldwide conflict which would continue for four years, bring death to 54.8 million and involve 57 nations.

Milpitans marched off to war in Europe and the Pacific, and the community's Japanese were ordered to relocation camps in Wyoming.

Hundreds vied for housing as Milpitas became a bedroom community for workers in the shipyards in the Richmond area to the north.

New businesses joined the oldtimers along Main Street. These included the Associated Seed Growers, Frank J. Gomes' (later Tom Cardoza's) Milpitas Feed and Appliance Store, Abner Newby's and Ray Barnes' gas stations, Charles G. Dominick's liquor store, Mamie Moretti's beauty shop, Anthony Roderick's auto repair business, Thomas T. Rose's Rose Valley Produce Co., Joseph and Anna Alves' groceries and meats, Joseph Turturici's shoe repair.

Raymond Madruga joined F.J. Terra in the blacksmith and farm implement firm, Cavino Rodriquez had a soft drink parlor, and Renselaer J. Smith, Jr., son of the long-time Milpitas doctor, was operating a fruit store. Robert McLaren was doing a booming business at the Fat

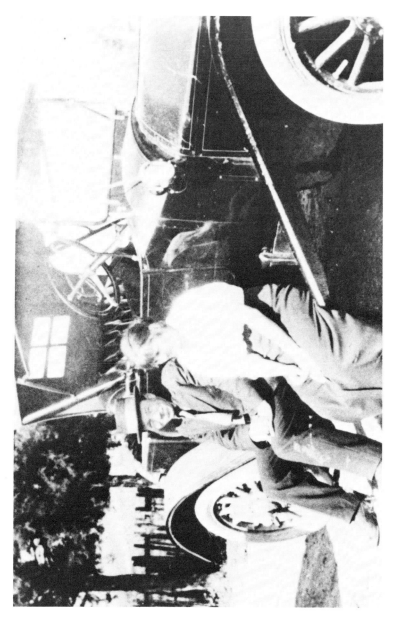

Mr. and Mrs. E. O. (Sandy) Wool 1915 shortly after their marriage. Wool family photo.

Boy Barbeque, a favorite stopping place for travelers.

Rationing of food, tires and gasoline, planting of "Victory" gardens, and frequent blackouts marked the war years, but probably had less impact on rural Milpitas.

Attendance at little Laguna School dropped below the required five pupils and the 78-year-old country school was closed in 1943. Mrs. Naomi Pinard was the last teacher.

John Carlos Rose, Gerry Ferry and Ben Rodgers served terms as postmasters and Al Currlin was the town's only doctor.

A major real estate transaction was the sale of the 2,585-acre Downing ranch in 1940 to a Los Angeles investment company, and its purchase three years later by general contractor Vance B. Minnis and his wife.

By this time, competition had made production of early peas in the foothill portion of the Downing ranch unprofitable and the many little houses once occupied by tenant farmers were empty.

E.O. (Sandy) Wool was Milpitas' representative on the County Board of Supervisors during the 1940s, and William Weller Curtner, grandson of two of Milpitas' earliest residents, Henry Curtner and Joseph Rush Weller, was a member of the County Planning Commission.

In the first days after Pearl Harbor, National Guard headquarters issued a call for unlimited enlistments, the county's aircraft warning system swung into action, Moffett Field authorities ordered all men to their posts, Permanente's giant magnesium and cement plant, one of the nation's top defense firms, was blacked out, and county agencies were ordered to keep watch for possible breakouts of racial riots.

It was a sad day late in May, 1942, when Milpitans of Japanese extraction boarded trains for relocation camps. Among those living in Milpitas when the order came to leave their homes and farms were Shigio Masunaga, Rikizo Matsui, I. Oyama, T. Takeda and Yuwakichi Sakauye.

The latter came to the Santa Clara Valley early in the

1900s and farmed on Trimble and Jacklin roads.

Sakauye's son, Eiichi (Edward), who was born in Milpitas, remembers May 30, 1942, when the family boarded the train at the old freight depot in San Jose.

"The shades were pulled down and there were two guards on each end (of the train). We didn't know where we were going. All night long we rode the train and the next morning we landed at Santa Anita race track," Edward Sakauye recalled in an interview 30 years later.

"We were ordered to line up and open our luggage," he said, remembering the Japanese evacuees were allowed to take "whatever we could carry with two hands," and "we had a duffle bag and a suitcase."

Officials checked for weapons, ration cards and contraband, Sakauye said.

They were taken to barracks and issued cots and some had mattresses, "but most got sacks to fill with straw. I had hay fever and I couldn't stand straw, so I slept without it. It was cold."

A total of 2, 847 county Japanese ·Americans were evacuated to the camps in Arizona, Wyoming, Tule Lake and other inland locations. Many were forced to sell their homes and businesses, most at giveaway prices, and others leased their lands until their return.

The Sakauye family was luckier than some. A neighbor cared for their land and turned it over to them after the war. The neighbor was returning a favor, remembering how the Sakauye family had cared for his dying mother when he was shipped overseas to fight in World War I.

Returning in 1945, the Sakauye family continued to develop one of the fine pear orchards that dotted the land between Alviso and San Jose, until at the time of this writing the pear trees were being replaced by the concrete and glass of the booming Silicon Valley's industrial growth.

It was estimated some 110,000 Japanese-Americans in Pacific coastal areas were sent to internment camps. Two-thirds of these were U.S. citizens who lost an estimated $400 million in property, of which the government in the mid-1950s repaid $38.5 million.

Returning Milpitas servicemen founded the Veterans' Club and one of its first projects was dedication of a World War II memorial erected in front of the grammar school on Main Street. The 1946 monument bore the names of 10 Milpitas area veterans who lost their lives in the war: Melvin Duarte, Melvin Garcia, Sebastian Ferreira, John Falcato, Herman Perry, Albert Vargas, Gerald Ferreira, William Rodriques, Tony Guerrero and Manuel Mattos.

The club built a hall in 1949, using lumber from a barracks purchased from Camp Shoemaker. The Veterans Hall stood on Main Street on a site originally owned by Tom Cardoza. It was later a pizza parlor and was eventually moved to make room for the Calaveras Boulevard overpass.

In the late 1940s Almshouse inmates began sharing their quarters with County Jail prisoners, the beginning of a move that in the 1950s would take over the entire facility for an expanded County Jail Farm.

As a jail farm the name became Elmwood, reportedly the suggestion of Milpitas physician, Dr. Albert Currlin, who chose the name because of the many huge elm trees on the grounds. An effort to have the Almshouse renamed "Rest Haven" had gone astray in the early 1930s when a Los Gatos couple complained the name was the same as that of their hotel.

In 1949 the bones of five adults and a child who had roamed the area before the white man came were uncovered in the huge shell mound between the Oakland Road and the Almshouse buildings, and in 1951 a pair of University of California archeologists spent several weeks digging

Frank Garcia. Elaine Rodgers photo.

into the ancient Indian encampment.

Across the nation in 1946 strikes idled some 4.6 million workers due to the rising wage demands in the face of runaway prices for consumer goods. In 1947 widespread food shortages had President Harry Truman urging meatless and eggless days for Americans. In 1948 inflationary wage boosts continued and the cost-of-living index reached an all-time high.

Major events in Milpitas in 1948 were formation of County Sanitation District No. 8 to furnish the area with modern sewage facilities, the Milpitas Development Association and the Volunteer Fire Department.

The fire department officially took over responsibility for fire protection of Milpitas and its environs June 30, 1948, with Joe Smith as chief. There were 16 firemen and one fire truck.

The development group immediately took up the issue of the Big Smell wafting over from San Jose's dump and hog farm to the northwest. The association lost little time in registering a formal complaint with the County Supervisors and San Jose City Council.

Police protection was still provided by the Sheriff's office, water was obtained from private wells, no subdivisions had been built, and the land out from Main Street was still in farms.

In 1949 typical prices paid by Milpitans included gasoline at 25 cents a gallon, cigarettes at 12 cents a pack, eggs 80 cents a dozen, bread 15 cents a loaf, and a two-bedroom home could be bought for $10,000.

In this year the old Laguna School was auctioned for $575 to rancher Mildred Beans who used it as a barn.

Milpitas Grammar School was bulging at the seams with no money available to build a new one. The only other grammar school serving the area was Airpoint up in the east hills. The closest high school was still in San Jose.

110

Milpitas Grammar School band. Elaine Rodgers photo.

Chapter XI

As Milpitas entered the decade of the 1950s, the little community was being caught up in the post-war growth that had come to California.

The citizens were becoming involved in county issues and in community projects, but the changes were gradual and almost imperceptible.

Milpitas was still the market place for the farmers and ranchers, and Main Street was still "downtown."

In 1950 the town boasted some 800 people, but the area served had nearly 4,200, more than half of whom lived on farms, according to a study made by the Santa Clara County Planning Commission.

There were 2,700 acres of orchards, 2,471 acres of truck farming, 311 acres in dairying, and 4,500 acres in dry farming.

The 1950 study showed 1,164 dwelling units, 476 with no private bath and 306 with no running water.

On Feb. 27, 1951, Milpitas residents voted for a $75,000 bond issue to help finance a sewage treatment plant for County Sanitation District No. 8. The vote was 196 in favor and 11 against the proposal, and it was not to be until 1954 that the sewers went into operation.

The Hetch Hetchy pipeline was being extended from Alameda County down to Milpitas and then west across Santa Clara County to the hills behind Stanford University. It was completed in December 1951 at a cost of $4,000,000, and would bring 75,000,000 gallons of Sierra water a day to residents along its route.

The phenomenal growth that was to come with the announcement in 1953 the Ford Motor Co. would build its plant in Milpitas, and the city's incorporation in January, 1954, was not even a dream as the little community closed out its first century in 1952.

Over the past 100 years the wilderness noted by the Spanish explorers and the gold rush pioneers had been cleared by plows and crosscut saws, and the plains cut into farms and orchards and fields planted to hay and grain.

The oldest landmarks had been replaced, but little changed.

The Mission Road still stretched north and south, and Calaveras Road ran down from the eastern hills to join the road to Alviso. The Higuera and Alviso adobes remained part of the landscape, and there were still folks named Parks, Abel, Curtner, Murphy, Winsor, Sepulveda, Rose and Zanker living in the area.

Oldtimers were still able to pick out the farms of Jacklin, Evans, Dixon, Trimble, Weller and Dempsey, whose names had been preserved on roads that criss-crossed the flatland and climbed into the hills.

Ranchers still drove their cattle down from the hills to pasture in the flats or to corrals at the depot, and many of the roads remained unpaved.

Deer continued to came down from the hills to sample the fruit and vegetables and coyotes yelped at the moon in the hills surrounding the little valley now covered by Calaveras Lake.

In the spring the pink and white blossoms of ancient fruit trees once again marked the site of vanished homesteads along Marsh and Felter roads, and here and there remained traces of old wagon roads.

In the fall the black oaks and maples turned red and gold in the canyon below Laguna Valley and in the draws high above Calaveras Lake, and there was the fragrance of burning leaves in the orchards along Piedmont and Oakland roads.

There was no local government, only the county, the state, and the nation, and the only times Milpitans got

113

together as a community were on occasions such as the Fourth of July, annual picnics, Portuguese fiestas and Memorial Day doings.

There was little major crime in those first 100 years. Even youngsters pretty much stayed out of any real trouble. After all, it wasn't too smart in a small community where everybody knew everyone, and you knew that your folks had heard of your escapade long before you got home to take the consequences.

There were no playgrounds and no planned recreation programs. Children made their own fun. There was always hunting and fishing, and it wasn't all that far to hike into San Jose or over to Alum Rock canyon where one could take the electric cars into the city. In the summer there were family outings to Santa Cruz and Capitola.

The years went slowly. Generations of the same families lived on the same land and farmed the same crops. New families came and bought the grocery store or the farm and continued in the same business.

Even along Main Street change was slow. The ratio of saloons and blacksmith shops stayed about the same, along side the hotel, the Catholic Church, the grammar school, the lumberyard and the doctor's office.

As Milpitas's first century ended the oldtimers could look back on the kind of changes that were normal with the passing years, but none could visualize the changes that would come almost overnight to turn the little one-street community into a sprawling city, and the countryside from hayfields and "little cornfields" to homes and industrial plants.

114

Vignettes

Mabel Mattos recalls:

"My father, Antone Vierra Silva, who was born on the Downing ranch, drove teams of mules for the (San Francisco) water company as a teenager before he went to Madera during World War I to go into the dairy business.

"He remembered the steam shovel they hauled up to build Calaveras Dam.

"He worked in the Milpitas cannery when he was a boy and one September when he was 11 the school authorities came to the cannery to round up the kids for school. My dad was tall for his age and he stood on a fruit box behind some machinery and they passed him by."

There were several large Silva families in Milpitas. . . six to eight children named Manuel, Tony, Rosie, Mary, Annie, Joe and Frank, so to keep the families straight the parents had nicknames. . . . There were the Domingues (Sunday) Silvas, the Antone (Mathias) Silvas, the Joseph (Pine) Silvas, the Joseph and Frank (Pacheco) Silvas, and Manuel (Four Bit) Silvas.

"The latter got his name because he always had 'four bits' in his pocket," Mabel says, but another story is that he offered four bits for whatever he bought.

Weller Curtner, descendant of pioneers Henry Curtner and Joseph Rush Weller, was a member of the Santa Clara County Planning Commission for 28 years, historian, story-teller with a marvelous memory of the way Milpitas area looked in "the old days".

"At the corner of Weller Road and Calaveras Road there was an Amish family by the name of Matthews and he had a blacksmith shop in there. He did the blacksmith work for the local men up there and his wife helped him. He'd beat a tattoo on the anvil and his wife would come out and strike for him. Swing a 14-pound sledge like a man.

"Those were the people that built the stone walls that you find up along the top of the ridges. In the fall when the crops were off they would go out with stone boats made out of a couple of willow trees about 10 inches in diameter that bent up a little bit in front and had some planks across.

"They cleared the land (of rock) and built the fence at the same time...the same as they did in New England."

On the history of the Portuguese.....

"Mostly they were whalers that had jumped ship in San Francisco. They were encouraged to jump ship by their captains because (the ships) had their barrels full of oil and a full load and they didn't want to take (the men) back to the Azores Islands.

"So when boats came in they (Portuguese crewmen) would get as much money as they could out of the captain and when they hit the ground they started traveling inland. The old captain went out with just enough crew to get back to the Azores where some stayed but others wanted to back to New Bedford and Boston and that's why there's a Portuguese song 'Take me around to New Bedford'."

Curtner's grandfather hired many of these early Portuguese to chop wood, raise vegetables..all hand work...potatoes all dug by hand. Packs hung down their backs from the shoulders...."

Illustrating the great strength of some of these men, Curtner recalled "old man Betemes" who wagered he could pack two sacks of potatoes up the hill on "my grandfather Curtner's place in Warm Springs without stopping".

"They (the other workers) put those sacks on his shoulders and he packed them up the hill half a mile...240 to 260 pounds".

"The first artichokes that I ate were brought in from the Stanford Ranch (later Hidden Valley at Warm Springs). Young Josiah Stanford had a trip to the Mediterranean and brought back some seeds and planted them over here.

"Stanford brought us the chokes in the backpack of his saddle. That was long before you could find an artichoke (grown commercially) in the valley."

Joe Smith, native of Warm Springs, came to Milpitas in 1930 and was the community's first fire chief in 1947. He

116

farmed in the foothills when first coming to the area.

"The ranchers and business people put up the money to buy the first fire truck. We had no tax money then and so they collected, I think it was $2,500, and went out and bought the old one we called "Lena" from a man by the name of Headburg from San Jose.

"The little house that we used was the Fat Boy garage and we developed that...raised it up a little higher and put a tower on it with a siren, and extended it either five or six feet so the truck would fit in it. That's where the bicycle shop is now (1980).

"Ben Rodgers was the assistant fire chief and we had 23 volunteers. We had an automatic signal that started the siren and when a call could come in our phone would start the siren. When the bell would ring we would all rush out there, throwing down our aprons or whatever we were doing, and run to the fire truck.

"We lived across the street from the fire house. I'd get all the information and by the time they (the volunteers) would be there I'd run out and we'd take off.

"We were our own independent Milpitas Fire District (before the city was incorporated)."

The Navy took over the area where the Sunnyhills tract was later built and had a training center there during the war, Smith recalls. "We used to get quite a few calls for rescue and stuff. They (the planes) would come down every once in a while. The leading instructor was the movie actor Jimmie Stewart. Emma (Mrs. Joe Smith) got to wait on him at Smith's Corners in the restaurant."

Dr. Al Currlin, native of San Jose, lived in Oakland before coming to Milpitas in 1935 "when Milpitas was still a shopping center for an agricultural community.

"There were around 1,400 to 1,500 hundred (people in the area...raised a lot of crops in the hills, cattle in the mountains and orchards down on the flat). I bought a little house on Main Street and it served as both home and office. I bought the whole thing for $2,000, nothing down and $25 month.

"I guess the first thousand or 1,500 babies I delivered were delivered at home, but this all changed when World War II came along. We just couldn't deliver babies at home anymore, it took too much time. It was in San Jose and O'Connor hospitals, and the main problem was in getting a bed because the population had increased. We had people stacked in the hallways and temporary barracks.

"Milpitas wasn't very big but percentage-wise it was big in Portuguese. I liked it there. I fell in love with the Portuguese people and by the time the war ended in late 1945, I didn't want to move.

"I guess Santa Clara, San Jose and Milpitas were the three largest in Central California in what they call the Holy Ghost Fiestas. They'd last two or three days, and on the last day, Sunday, they'd close off Main Street (San Jose-Oakland Highway) and it was just up to traffic to find its way around back roads for an hour or two while they held the parade which would wind up at the church with a big barbecue and all kinds of things."

Josephine Simas Carlo, native of Milpitas, one of 11 children of a Portuguese whaler, Joseph Simas, and Mary Frank, native Californian born in the Mother Lode mining town of Rough and Ready. Her father came to the area in the 1880s and had a grocery store and barber shop. Josephine married Al Carlo in 1936 and 10 years later they bought the Kozy Kitchen restaurant on Main Street.

"I went to work in the Bayside cannery in Alviso at the age of 14...I told them I was 16. The cannery truck would pick up workers in Milpitas and in the hills, and bring them home again.

"We worked from sunrise to sunset, six days a week, during the season.

118

"Bayside canned apricots, peaches, pears, string beans. My first job was hand-pitting fruit, and later I operated a peeling machine.

"Cannery owner Tom Foo Chew was good to his workers. His girls worked like we did. There was a dance every week and a big party at the end of the year with tables of food and dancing.

"When the tide came in we sometimes worked up to our knees in water, and sometimes had to wait until the tide went out, then come back to work at 11 at night.

"I never worked in the pea cannery in Milpitas, but I remember the peas hauled down from the hillsides in wagons. We children used to sit by the side of the road and eat the fresh peas that fell off the wagons. It must have been on Saturdays because peas came in the spring when we were in school."

Mary Prada came to Milpitas in 1952, at the end of the 100-year period this history covers, she and her husband Joseph, bought 37 acres on Evans Road, which included the old home of the Josiah Evans family, pioneers of the early 1850s.

"I was born in the Azores Islands and lived there until I was 10 years old. My father had come to California years before and worked on an Evans Road ranch. Every ship that came in would be hats or shoes or clothing or candy (sent by her father). I began to think there was no other place like Milpitas because nobody else had these things. Every night I would go to bed and say, 'Dear God, I hope that some day I can go to California and to Evans Ranch.'

It was May of 1912 we (mother, Mary and her sister) came to California. We had two uncles who were farming the Evans ranch, too. We stayed in a hotel in San Jose and the next morning we dressed up and got on the train and came to Milpitas.

"I thought Milpitas would be the most beautiful place

119

in the world and when the train stopped at the station and my father said 'we're getting off here', I didn't see anything. Uncle Manuel came to get us in the spring wagon. There were no seats and we had to climb up onto the bed (of the wagon) and sit there.... my beautiful dress, I didn't want it to get dirty.

"We went up Calaveras Road. The fields were green but I didn't see any beautiful buildings".

Lupe "Louie" Lugo, for some 60 years a cowboy on the Lee Ogier ranch in the back country east of Calalveras reservoir, remembered when "there wasn't a fence between the ranch and the San Joaquin Valley". He helped to build some that still poke through the poison oak and cascara across the Diablo range.

"Once six of us built seven miles of fence in two weeks," Lugo recalled in an interview years later, and he remembered wild horses in the area.

Lugo was one of the oldtime story tellers with a fine sense of humor. One of his favorites, which he swore was true and probably was, concerned his pet steer (neutered bull) which he used to ride.

"He (the steer) was out with a bunch of cows in a field and was acting pretty friendly with the cows. People got excited so I rode him home.

"A few days later a city slicker (Lugo knew alot of these), comes along with his cow and wants to breed her to by "bull". I said 'sure', and he left her all day. When he came to get her, I didn't say anything. He didn't offer to pay any breeding fee, which was just as well."

Ray Madruga was born in 1919 in his grandfather's house where Calaveras overpass was built in more recent years, and who is related to several prominent Milpitans, including Joe Smith, Frank Pedro, and Frank J. Terra. His grandfather, Frank P. Terra, owned property on Winsor Street where Ray and Frank J. Terra built the building used for many years as a post office.

Ray remembers the growers' market where people brought produce. He says A.P. Giannini hauled produce from the Milpitas market to Alviso to be shipped by boat to San Francisco.

Ray said he and the Terras repaired much of the equipment used on farms in the Milpitas area. There was lots of haying and truck crops, and they sold and repaired the Knapp side hill plow manufactured in San Jose.

Ray's dad worked on the Soares dairy where K-Mart was built in recent years, and there were still dairy buildings there when Milpitas was incorporated.

Sal Cracolice remembers the baseball teams that played about where the old entrance to the Almshouse (County Jail Farm) was. Joe Stemel and Auston Pelton were a couple of the managers of the Milpitas team when Sal was playing second or third base in the late 1920s.

"We won more than we lost. Every Sunday afternoon the whole town would be there to see the team play San Jose, Berryessa, Santa Clara or any of the area teams."

Sal was also a bike rider when in his late teens before he moved to Milpitas from San Jose. His last race was "from San Jose's old city hall up the peninsula back of Palo Alto, to Half Moon Bay and back over the mountain to South San Francisco and south to Bay Meadows where there was horse racing and where Jackie Coogan was making a motion picture, called "Get Your Hair Cut".

121

Gene Vennum, born in Berryessa and the grandson of O.H.P. Vennum, who was the first justice of the peace of Milpitas township, had some memories of his school days.

He attended old Eagle School in Berryessa, which he pointed out was typical of all the one-room schools of the years before and after World War I...."a large building set on a one-acre lot with a privy in each back corner, one for the boys and the other for the girls, and both four-hole affairs.

"By the time I got to them in 1913 they were scarred. Every boy owned a pocket knife, and most of these knives were used on seats, walls, and what-have-you," Vennum remembered, "and besides initials carved inside a heart, peep holes sometimes showed up in an outhouse wall."

He recalled the privy was furnished with newspaper or Sears Roebuck catalogues, and every so often "one of the bigger boys would set fire to the building by dropping a lighted piece of paper down the hole.

"This sort of thing was ruinous to the olfactory nerves (not to mention the outhouse) and if the arsonist was caught, woe be unto him".

Jack Wool, retired Wool Cannery executive and nephew of the late E.O. (Sandy) Wool, remembers driving cattle to market from his uncle's ranch high up on Weller Road in 1927.

"We drove the cattle down Calaveras Road to Dempsey and then south on Dempsey. Both of these roads were fenced and the cattle moved right along. But we ran out of fence below Dempsey Road and the cattle got out into the orchards. It was hard on the trees and the orchardists were mad.

"The police stopped traffic on the Oakland Road so we could get the cattle across the Coyote Creek bridge. We pushed them down to Gish Road and over to Nelson's meat company."

The Parks family was the chief reason for Oak Ridge School back on the mountain above the Arroyo Honda, according to the family.

Mark Parks used to claim that when the last Parks kid got old enough to work on the farm and quit school, classes were over for everybody, and the school was torn down.

The family ran cattle in the remote country east of Milpitas from the 1880s up into the 1950s. Jack Parks, who died in 1951, never missed voting in an election, riding horseback the 35 miles down to Milpitas to cast his ballot.

Sam Parks had the hotel in Milpitas for several years early in this century, but after the 1906 earthquake went back to the hills' "where it's safer".

Mrs. Gladys Farnsworth Berger of San Jose taught at Laguna School from 1931 to 1939 and remembers "there weren't enough children to keep the school open so I took my three."

Her youngest was the school's only first grader when Mrs. Berger began teaching at Laguna and she said "when the little one was taking her nap the other children would be very quiet."

One of Mrs. Berger's pupils was Johnny Covo, later a successful rancher on Felter Road.

"There weren't too many deer when I was a kid," remembers **John Covo,** who grew up on the Felter Road ranch where he still lives.

"Most of the ranches ate deer meat throughout the winter. When they needed a piece of meat they went out and got it. There were a lot of private ranches then, and deer were scarce. They came back after the (San Francisco) water company closed their lands to hunting.

"There were lions, but I've seen more in the last four or five years than in my whole life.

"There have always been coyotes, and now there are a lot of wild pigs. The coyotes have cut down the squirrel population, and they get a lot of fawns."

123

Florence Lee (Ogier) Hawley's story about her uncle, Sam Ayer:

"The sun was almost down and he would be late for supper, but the little boy wasn't in any hurry. The hills above Milpitas were covered with poppies and lupines; the birds were singing and Sam (Ayer) was happily riding his very first horse. True, it wasn't as big as some, and his big sisters laughed and said it was only a pony. But it was really a little horse. Mamma said so, and she was always right.

"Lupe would be cooking supper, and if he hurried perhaps she would tell him a story of the old days like the one she told last week about the cemetery. Could it be that dead people came out of their graves after the sun set?

"Just then Sam realized that he was going to ride by the old Laguna cemetery that was overgrown and really spooky. He jogged around the corner and there it was. Perhaps it was wise to go faster. Something hazy and gray wavered in the dim light and the hairs prickled on his neck as a coyote howled and the bushes rustled.

"It was too much for a 7-year-old. He kicked his little horse, squished his eyes tight shut and they went by the cemetery at top speed — and kept on running down Calaveras Road.

"In later years Sam said that for a long time after that, he always shut his eyes when he passed that cemetery. After all, Lupe always told the truth and what 7-year-old wants to see a ghost."

Index

126

130

131

Bibliography

Arbuckle, Clyde, **Santa Clara County Ranchos,** Harlan-Young Press, 1968.

Barrett, Dick, **Dick Barrett '67,** Harlan-Young Press, San Jose, 1967.

The American Heritage History of the 20s and 30s, American Heritage Publishing Co., New York, 1970.

Gilbert H. Kneiss, **Bonanza Railroads,** Stanford University Press, 1941.

Daley, Edith, **War History of Santa Clara County,** Santa Clara County Historical Society, 1919.

Doten, Alfred, **The Journals of Alfred Doten, 1849-1903,** edited by Walter Van Tilburg Clark, University of Nevada Press, 1973.

Foot, H.S., editor, **Pen Pictures from the Garden of the World,** Lewis Publishing Co., Chicago, 1888.

Guinn, J.M., **Coast Counties of California,** Chapman Publishing Co., Chicago, 1904.

Hall, Frederic, **The History of San Jose and Surroundings,** A.L. Bancroft & Co., San Francisco, 1871.

Cleland, Robert Glass, **California, The American Period,** MacMillan Co., New York, 1939.

Federal Writers' Project, WPA, **California A Guide to the Golden State,** Hastings House, publishers, New York, 1939.

Craig, Madge, **History of Milpitas.** Milpitas School District, publishers.

Hom, Gloria S., editor, **Chinese Argonauts,** Foothill Community College District, 1971

Abeloe, William N., revised edition of **Historic Spots in California,** Stanford University Press, 1966

The Country Club of Washington Township Research Committee, **History of Washington Township,** third edition, 1950-1965.

James W.F. and G.H. McMurry, **History of San Jose,** Smith Printing Co., San Jose, 1933.

Mars, Amaury, **Reminiscences of Santa Clara Valley and San Jose,** Mysell-Rollins, Co., San Francisco, 1901.

Milpitas Post

Munro-Fraser, J.P., **History of Santa Clara County,** Alley, Bowen & Co., San Francisco, 1881.

San Jose and Santa Clara County directories, 1870 to 1952.

San Jose Patriot, San Jose Mercury, San Jose Daily Herald, San Jose Evening News, San Jose Times-Mercury, San Jose Mercury News.

Sawyer, Eugene T., **History of Santa Clara County,** Historic Record Co., Los Angeles, 1922.

Shortridge, Charles M., **Santa Clara County and Its Resources (Sunshine, Fruit and Flowers A Souvenir of the San Jose Mercury, 1895,** San Jose Mercury Publishing and Printing Co., San Jose, 1895.

Thompson & West, **Historical Atlas Map of Santa Clara County, 1876,** San Francisco, 1876.

Trager, James, editor, **The People's Chronology, A Year-By-Year Record of Human Events from Prehistory to the Present,** Holt, Rinehart and Winston, New York, 1979.

Planning Department, Santa Clara County, **Milpitas, an arrested community meets the 20th century,** 1954.

California State Earthquake Investigation Commission, April 18, 1906, Washington, D.C., Carnegie Institution of Washington, 1908-1910.

Great Register of Santa Clara County, 1877 and 1888.